Who Are You?

MEGAN HENLEY

Who Are You?

WITH ONE CLICK
SHE FOUND HER
PERFECT MAN.

AND HE FOUND
HIS PERFECT VICTIM.

Certain details in this story, including names, places and dates, have been changed to protect the family's privacy.

HarperElement
An imprint of HarperCollins*Publishers*
1 London Bridge Street
London SE1 9GF

www.harpercollins.co.uk

First published by HarperElement 2016

1 3 5 7 9 10 8 6 4 2

© Megan Henley 2016

Megan Henley asserts the moral right to be identified as the author of this work

A catalogue record of this book is available from the British Library

ISBN 978-0-00-814433-3

Printed and bound in Great Britain by Clays Ltd, St Ives plc

MIX
Paper from
responsible sources
FSC
www.fsc.org
FSC° C007454

FSC™ is a non-profit international organisation established to promote the responsible management of the world's forests. Products carrying the FSC label are independently certified to assure consumers that they come from forests that are managed to meet the social, economic and ecological needs of present and future generations, and other controlled sources.

Find out more about HarperCollins and the environment at www.harpercollins.co.uk/green

For Wugsa and Weeves: you are all that matter x

CONTENTS

PROLOGUE

The message was clear. Horribly, terrifyingly clear.

> You need to get out, Megan. Take the kids and run. They're
> watching you. If you don't listen to Vic, his dad will kill you
> and the girls. You know they've been after you for a while,
> but he can't stop them anymore. He has tried his best – he
> has fought for you and done things no man should ever have
> to even consider – he's put himself on the line time and time
> again. But the time has come. Trust me – Val x

Valerie had been on my side for so long. She was always
there when I needed to chat online, always there with a
supportive message, or – like now – words of warning.
I was living in the middle of a nightmare. My partner,
Vic, had taken on the anger of his entire family by
continuing to have a relationship with me, and now it
was coming to a head.

His whole family was violent, with his father the worst of the bunch. He had been brought up among Romany gypsies, his parents at the top of the hierarchy, always willing to do what they needed to stay in that position, never shy of dishing out violence and hatred when they saw fit. They were unpredictable and lawless. They wanted me dead, they wanted my babies dead. They had their own rules and no one could talk them out of what they planned to do to us.

Vic had broken away from it all and they despised him for it. He had been punished and threatened, stalked and beaten. He wanted nothing to do with it all, but he kept being drawn back in by family loyalty one way or another. He had lost too many friends and too many years.

But worse than anything, he was with me – a gorja, a non-gypsy, a woman who was the lowest of the low. We had a child together, we wanted a life, a future free of the intimidation and terror that came from being a gypsy king's son who had turned his back on the privilege and horror that came with that role. It looked like we would never have it; it looked like this could be the end.

I knew, from all of the stories Vic had told me, that the gang now looking for me and my two little girls wouldn't hesitate to murder us, just as they had shown no hesitation when killing so many others. They operated outside the rules which governed normal society, beyond the reach of the law – no one would touch them – and they were on a mission to get us. They were contract killers, mercenaries, who wouldn't flinch from carrying out his father's orders. I was nothing to them or to the gypsy king, my daughter wasn't seen as his blood – we were scum, and he wanted us eradicated.

Vic had been away from the house for some time. He'd thought his absence would distract his dad, that if he was away we would be safer, but I wasn't so sure. I couldn't sleep, even though I'd been assured that protection was in place. I knew that I was being followed everywhere I went and that the house was being watched the whole time, but the lines were blurred.

I wasn't sure who the good guys were any more.

In fact, I knew that the good guys did their share of killing anyway, so who could I trust?

Valerie.

I could trust her. She had been there for me from the start, she only had my best interests and the interests of my two little girls at heart. She was an honest, strong woman who knew Vic's story and knew that this time, more than ever before, he simply had to win.

I started to pack, throwing a few things into bags, concentrating on what the kids would need, wondering where I could go with the dogs and cats in tow as well. Vic had been warning me for so long now that the girls were in danger, that they would be used to send a message. The rest of my family wasn't safe either. I was aware that if I went to my mum's I could be leading the killers to her. Where could I go?

There was nowhere.

I stopped. I was shaking but I also knew that I couldn't really leave, despite Valerie's words. Vic had told me to stay – and there was a good reason behind him wanting me to do that. We couldn't go on like this. There had been so many threats, so many warnings.

It was us or them.

I could hardly believe that my life had come to this. I was an intelligent, successful woman when I met him, the mother of a beautiful daughter. I had a good education behind me and a thriving business ahead. How had I become part of this world? A world that spoke of murder as if it was nothing, of revenge killings and contracts and mutilation and torture? I'd do anything to protect my girls, but I felt powerless. Everything was out of my control and Vic was the only one who could save us.

My mind was going at a million miles an hour, my heart was pounding. I just wanted to make sure we were all safe, I had to believe that we could be. I couldn't waste time wondering how I'd got to this point, how awful it was, and how many threats were out there.

We just had to survive.

I couldn't bear to think of the alternative.

CHAPTER 1

TEENAGE KICKS

Childhood – October 2008

I hadn't felt settled for a long time. Life hadn't been easy for a while, but I wasn't silly enough to ignore the fact that a lot of that was down to silly teenage decisions and the pigheadedness that sometimes took over. Taking responsibility for your actions is awfully grown-up, but I was starting to realise that it was something I needed to do. I wasn't a bad kid, but, in retrospect, I think I was a pretty frustrating one. I'm sure my parents would have said it had all started with my period of teenage rebellion; a period in my life which had resulted in Ruby. While she was, without doubt, the best thing that had ever happened to me, falling pregnant to a man who would never settle down hadn't exactly been what I expected, or what was expected of me.

I was the second oldest of four children, and the only girl. We were lucky enough to grow up on a 500-acre farm near the village of Cowfold in Sussex, which had been in my father's family for over a hundred years. It was an idyllic setting for a lovely childhood. The farm felt as if it was in my DNA; I knew every inch of the impressive six-bedroom farmhouse, and the land surrounding it. My childhood memories were gorgeous ones of times spent building dens out of hay bales and corrugated iron, playing Pooh sticks on the bridge over the river, and galloping at breakneck speeds across stubble fields on one of the many ponies that came and went. I loved animals and I loved being outdoors. Summers felt as if they would never end, and I remember those days as being full of laughter and freedom. My dad was a busy farmer, and not exactly 'hands on' with us kids. Maybe things were more like that back then – there were traditional ways to be for some men. His hard-working lifestyle meant that he rarely had time to sit around and play, and he wasn't an emotional sort of man, always checking up on how we felt. Mum was a local politician, a short, round, feisty woman of Irish descent, who suffered no fools. She was warmer to us, and the one we went to for support and cuddles, but she was also the sort of person who instilled hard rules and values in me and my brothers from an early age. She very much believed that you made your bed and that was where you lay. They had done well for themselves through hard work and strong beliefs – we wanted for nothing really, and I don't think I knew how lucky I was.

Despite my fortunate surroundings, it was a lonely upbringing. I didn't get on that well with my older brother – our only interaction seemed to be when he'd come up with a new way to torment me – and there was a large age gap between me and the younger ones. When I played on the farm and in the fields, it tended to be on my own. I had a vivid imagination and the time passed quickly, but I suppose I did yearn for someone to share it with. From the outside, we probably looked like a big, noisy, happy family, but there were definitely cracks there.

Going to school several miles away meant that I had no friends locally, and the farm was in the middle of nowhere, so I spent a lot of time with my own thoughts. Even when I was a little girl, I made a promise to myself that I would be a different sort of parent and give any children I had a different sort of life. I would play with them and be a really hands-on mum; they would always come first and I would never say I was too busy when they wanted to play or tell me something. Everything around me was beautiful but I was undoubtedly lonely. I had siblings and I had parents who gave me all the material things I could wish for, but there was something missing. I wanted a mum and dad who would play with me and draw and sing and dance and look for fairies and chase butterflies. I would be that sort of mum, I truly would.

In some ways, I wished my childhood away because of this. I couldn't wait until I was old enough to drive and had the freedom to escape. I would find the life I wanted, make it for myself and leave the loneliness behind. When I was old enough, I told myself, I would rush head first towards that life and never look back. I left school at sixteen, with good grades in my exams, and convinced my parents that I would be far happier at the local state-run college.

'School's not for me,' I remember telling them. 'They don't understand me – they don't see what I could do if they would just let me be myself. I can't breathe in that sort of environment. I need to be me.' It's been said by countless teenagers before, and will be heard by countless weary parents for the rest of time, but I genuinely believed it. 'I can't wait for ever,' I went on. 'I want to have a life, and I can't do it with all of those rules and people not being able to see what I'm really capable of.' I'm sure they must have rolled their eyes as I claimed I'd change the world. They were good people, they just had their own way of seeing things and, as a teenager, I naturally believed my way was far superior. What did they know? I could have the world at my feet if they would let me. I believed my own words. At that point, I really was telling them what I thought was the truth, and I felt no sadness whatsoever at leaving behind the world of school uniforms and weekend classes. I can't waste time thinking what my life would have been like if I had followed the path they wanted to set me; that way madness lies.

I was young and wanted to have a good time. It was the mid-1990s and the rave culture was in full swing. While most of the girls in the year I had left behind at school were into the Spice Girls, I was obsessed with the various sets of mix tapes from raves I'd been to. It was music I could relate to and I was obsessed with it. I would lie on my bed listening to the mixes for hours on end, with colourful flyers for clubs and raves covering every inch of my bedroom walls. So, when I left school, I needed to find people who felt the same. They must be out there, and I knew that if only I could track them down they could be part of my plan to be somebody.

'I'd die without music,' I told friends, seriously feeling that it was true and that *no one* had ever felt so intense or so switched on to life. It's hard now to remember that girl, but I know she was there for a while. Anyone who didn't see how important music was had no place in my life – how could anyone even survive without it?

For the next few years music was my life, just as I had claimed all along. I started at college, but only applied myself half-heartedly, living for the times when

I could go to raves or gigs. Education was just something to do; music was something to *be*. A-levels seemed so unimportant to me, and I had that teenage desire to make sure I fitted in with the right crowd, wore the right clothes, and said the right things to the people who impressed me, rather than actually do any work. My parents, especially Mum, were completely bewildered. They had, naturally, hoped that I would sort myself out once I left school, but there was little sign of that happening. All I wanted was music; all I was interested in was music. It didn't seem so daft any longer because I saw myself as a proper grown-up who could make proper grown-up choices – all I wanted to choose within that grown-up world was music.

I decided at the end of the spring term of my first year that college wasn't for me, which by a stroke of fortune (in my eyes) coincided with college deciding that I wasn't for them! Mum and Dad were furious, and told me I had to get a job. I heard the phrase 'You're wasting your life!' more than I wanted to, but, with the certainty of youth, I shrugged it off. They wanted me to get a job? Well, I'd get a job then. Within a few days of leaving college I had done exactly that, getting a full-time position at a motorway service station, flipping burgers in Wimpy; a curious occupation for a long-term vegetarian such as myself, but the only thing that had been advertised in the local paper that week. Mum and

Dad might have thought it would help me develop a sense of responsibility, but all that happened was that I now had the cash to go to gigs and raves whenever the fancy took me. My social life continued to buzz, and I now had more money in my pocket to fund it.

After a few months of working at Wimpy, I had another go at college, but the result was similar to the first time. During the spring term, shortly after my eighteenth birthday, I left college again and moved away from home. I was sick of my parents telling me what to do, and like so many teenagers before me, worked out that I knew everything and needed no one. I rented a flat, with my friend Gareth, in a sleepy little place on the edge of Horsham, which was where most of the friends I'd made at college lived. I had some inheritance money in the bank and a large group of close friends who were always up for a good time. A few of the girls I knew from college were working in a 'massage parlour' nearby, so between us there was always a steady flow of fun and the cash to fund it all. It was everything I'd hoped for when I'd made all my proclamations to my parents and I fully expected them to come round and eat humble pie at any moment.

The next step for me was to get some sort of job that would continue to bring in a bit of cash but not be something I'd do for the rest of my life – I wanted something better and more fulfilling than a dead-end office job, but I was happy enough to do it for a little while as a means to an end. I got a position in a dental lab. I had done all my word-processing qualifications at school, so that type of work was a logical move, as I wasn't qualified to do much else. The money was terrible, but after a few months I managed to get a better-paid position in the accounts department of a huge hotel booking agency. It was deadly boring and I never really committed to it. It wasn't working out quite as I'd hoped. I'd gone from bored and living at home, to bored at college, and now bored in a series of humdrum jobs. Part of me started to wonder if Mum and Dad were right – maybe I was wasting my life. I couldn't dwell on that depressing proposition for too long, though – I had the world to conquer.

When I turned nineteen I moved into a caravan, which initially was on my parents' farm. This was a decision driven, yet again, by money. Despite working full time I was hopeless at managing my finances, and so a life with no rent or bills to pay seemed like a fantastic idea; I was completely oblivious to responsibility and a bit of a brat really. Living in the caravan was meant to be a short-term option, but I soon got used to the cold winters and having to go outside to the loo, and it didn't make sense to move. I left my accounts job and became a van driver, delivering garage parts, which was much more my cup of tea as I was out and about unsupervised, flirting with guys at garages and driving, which were all enjoyable activities as far as I was concerned.

Looking back, I can't believe how many opportunities I threw away. I could have had the world at my feet by that stage just as I'd expected, especially given the environment I'd been raised in, but I was too short-sighted to see it. We all think about what would happen if we could turn back the clock – maybe I wonder more than most.

Just after I'd turned twenty-one, a friend called Tattoo Sue moved in with me after splitting up with her boyfriend. She was great fun to be around, and no trouble as a lodger. I was a sucker for a sad story or a bit of crying, and gave in to far too many people, but Sue was a really fantastic addition to my life and I loved her being there. She – obviously – lived up to her nickname, with tattoos over most of her body, and constant plans for more. She was funny and loud, and seemed to know everyone, but she was also a good influence on me. Hardly a day went past without her saying that there was someone I 'had' to meet, and the social side of my life became even more hectic. She was usually right about these people, and everyone she introduced me to was lovely – but, one day, Sue really hit the jackpot.

With the words 'Megan – meet Lucas' my world was changed for ever.

Lucas had been living on the road for more than twenty years, and the open-air lifestyle had done him good. He wasn't the backpacking type, more of a free spirit who wandered around wherever the fancy took him. He was two decades older than me, with handsome looks, wisdom and an engaging maturity. I thought he was absolutely perfect and couldn't believe it when he seemed to feel the same way about me. For that perfect moment I was just what he wanted, and I couldn't believe my luck.

Almost immediately, we were a couple. He was like no boyfriend I'd had before. I was completely captivated. Although the relationship seemed idyllic to me, looking back, it was probably incredibly clichéd. We would spend every night tangled up in each other, madly in love, obsessed, and afterwards I'd listen intently as Lucas delivered personal sermons on the ways of the world, the dangers of consumerism, and all of his other political beliefs. He was an ex-punk, anarchist biker turned New Age traveller – just the kind of boyfriend to give nightmares to parents.

Ironically, I settled down a bit when I was with him. Despite his constant lectures on the evils of capitalism, I went back to work – temping in various offices suited me as I could move on whenever I felt restless or annoyed, but I still had some money coming in. This way of life was a perfect way to combine my flighty nature with being able to pay the bills. However, there was a part of me that realised I was going to have to grow up at some point and achieve something in life. I signed up for a homeopathy degree and I immediately felt as if it was the right thing to do.

From the very first day, everyone was friendly. As we sat around the lake at lunchtime, eating sandwiches and getting to know each other, I made a random comment out of nowhere. 'I wonder how many people will have babies over the next four years before we graduate?'

Everyone laughed and joked about it, pointing out the ones who already had kids, or the ones who said they were keen to start a family.

I didn't think it would be me.

A couple of weeks later I was frozen in shock, staring at a positive pregnancy test. It was completely unplanned and not something Lucas and I had ever discussed, but terminating the pregnancy wasn't something I could contemplate. I felt that, unprepared emotionally and financially as I was, I couldn't deny this child a chance of life. It was meant to be.

Lucas felt differently. He already had two children with two different women and contributed nothing to their lives. From the moment I told him I was having a baby, he changed.

'If you really loved me, you'd get rid of it,' he told me one night after days of unrelenting pressure to think of the 'options'. 'We can't be tied down like this – we're soul mates, Megan; we can't be shackled. A baby means that you'd just be thinking about all the stuff that society tells you it needs. You'd have to work in jobs you hate – what would that do to you? There would be no more partying, you'd be a mum – that would be it, that would be your identity.'

I could see what he was saying, but I'd always wanted to be a great mum. If that meant making some compromises, I'd do it. I couldn't abort a child just because I fancied a night out every now and then. The baby would grow up with a love of music too, it would learn to be free and happy, and it would have a mother who would know how to make sure it never felt lonely. I would do well at this, I told myself, I would make sure my little one was the happiest, most loved child in the world.

The comments Lucas made changed everything, though. From that point, I assumed I would be a single parent, even if he did hang around for a bit longer. Nothing would make me kill my baby, no one would emotionally blackmail me into giving up this child. Throughout the pregnancy I kept thinking of all the promises I had made to myself about what sort of mother I would be one day, and I realised that 'one day' had arrived.

'This baby is happening,' I told Lucas. 'I don't really care whether you want it or not – the important thing is that I do, and I'll do all I can to make sure I'm the best mother I can possibly be.'

He shook his head. 'Suit yourself,' he muttered, and left the room.

The pregnancy became the 'elephant in the room' that neither of us really mentioned. It was ludicrous – as my skinny frame gained four stones of extra bulk, there was no missing my enormous belly, but still we never spoke about what was to come. We were both in denial. I sailed through the pregnancy physically. I was young and healthy, and had the ability to blank out what might happen after the little one arrived apart from the happy aspects of it all. I still spent most of my time listening to music and dancing. I'd sing to my bump, dance around the caravan and tell the baby what a lovely time we'd have together. That baby was surrounded by music all the time and I started to think I'd have a partner in crime, as it were. I'd teach it about all of the things that mattered to me. I could still take on the world – I'd just have a small person by my side to do it with.

I went into labour twelve days before my due date on a night when there was a huge red hunter's moon low in the sky. It was a beautiful sight and seemed like a wonderful omen, as if Nature was on my side. Leaving my confused-looking dog Maxie – who was just a little puppy at the time – staring out of the open caravan door, we got into my car, where I braced myself against the pain with my feet on the dashboard. Lucas was looking as if he hadn't quite realised a thing like this might happen, and I wondered just how much he had been able to block out. While I had been in denial to some extent too, it had really just related to never raising the issue of my pregnancy with my baby's father. I was the one who got huge, I was the one who was woken by kicking and heartburn, so it wasn't as if I could pretend I wasn't actually having a baby. Seeing Lucas's face now, as my contractions increased, I suspected he had actually told himself it wasn't happening at all. It must have been a huge shock to him to realise that, after nine months of pregnancy, a baby would actually arrive!

My labour was short and intense. At just after 4.30am I was holding my tiny daughter. I gazed at her perfect little face, her wide-set, slate blue eyes taking their first peep at the world, and I was mesmerised.

'Hello, Ruby,' I whispered. 'Are you ready for an adventure?'

This changed everything. This little person was the reason I was here. She was so little but so beautiful with lots of dark hair and pouty little lips that made her look like some sort of fairytale princess. I couldn't believe I had managed this. Flighty Megan Henley – a mum.

There was more relief flooding through me than just that of holding my baby – Lucas was choked up too, shedding tears of joy as I passed our daughter to him, before giving her a cuddle against his bare chest. Finally he knew this was real. It had taken a while, but we'd turned a corner. A very dramatic one!

Ruby had been born the day after the academic year ended. When I returned after summer, my tutors were all fine about the gorgeous ten-week-old bundle I took along to classes with me. It seemed blissful to start with, but reality soon set in – trying to concentrate on lectures and take notes whilst breastfeeding, having had little to no sleep, proved too much, and I left the course at Christmas. Becoming a mum had been a huge shock to my system. Luckily, from the word go Ruby was an angelic child, always content and placid. Even so, the daily grind, monotony and isolation of looking after a small baby was difficult; day in, day out I would be stuck in the caravan with Ruby and Maxie, who were not great conversationalists. After the first few weeks, where he stayed every night, Lucas only turned up every couple of days, a pattern which caused obvious friction between us. Our relationship soon began to fall apart. I desperately wanted things to work out, but it seemed we had hugely different expectations of the situation and there was no future in it for either of us. It didn't matter, I told myself, I could do it all, I could be everything and everyone for her.

Just after Ruby turned one, Lucas and I split up. I'd had to end it, for my sake as well as hers. He was constantly making nasty comments about my weight, even though I was far from obese. The only part he played in our lives was to turn up once or twice a week, expecting me to make dinner for him, and we never had sex together from the moment Ruby was born – his choice, not mine. I decided that things would never change and maybe if I ended it I would at least have a chance of happiness, which would never happen with him. I didn't want Ruby to grow up absorbing those sorts of messages, so I decided that both of us could do better.

They say it never rains but it pours, and not long after that the caravan became infested with mice and I had to face up to the fact that, for Ruby's sake more than anything, it was time to be 'normal'. I found a flat for us to rent, but it still wasn't ideal. We bounced between different places for a couple of years as the short-term lets became more and more unreliable, the landlords more and more unscrupulous, the lifestyle more and more depressing. Finally, a couple of miles outside Horsham, I found somewhere perfect, a cottage that screamed 'perfect family' to me. Mother, child, dog – we didn't need anyone else. It was hard, but maybe in this place with its pretty setting and huge potential, life would get easier.

Ruby had just turned three when we moved into the cottage where I'd hoped for security but where my life was about to be turned upside down. I was finding life quite hard, constantly struggling to make ends meet, even though I was juggling about four part-time jobs. Sometimes, once the bills were paid, there was very little money left for food – I always made sure that Ruby and Maxie were fed, but I didn't take such good care of myself.

I didn't intend to stay poor, any more than I had intended to get pregnant at twenty-two. I had to figure out of a way of making some money. I'd always loved antiques, so wondered if I could turn a hobby into something that would actually bring in some money. I began selling beautiful furniture, paintings and china online, and within a few months I had established a thriving business. I spent all of my spare time sourcing stock at car boot sales, charity shops, auctions, house clearances – usually with Ruby and Maxie in tow. I made contacts in lots of different countries and thoroughly enjoyed the new challenge. My timing was right too, as the demand for vintage and retro things was just kicking in.

With my financial woes easing, the next thing I needed to have some luck with was my love life. After a couple of ill-fated relationships since breaking up with Lucas, I decided to try internet dating. I took a deep breath and made my profile, creating what I hoped was a positive spin of myself and my situation, uploading my best photo, as everyone does. I was immediately surprised at the lack of effort and originality the average man was prepared to put in to his messages, and how many of them thought I wanted nothing more than to see pictures of what was in their knickers almost immediately, but within a week one did catch my eye. It was from a man called Christopher, who was from London and worked in the music business (that bit caught my eye straight away!). He was in his thirties, divorced and the father of three children. After a couple of weeks of chatting online, we arranged to meet for a drink, on a Sunday afternoon in London.

It was a freakishly hot day for October, so I pulled a summer dress out of hibernation for the occasion. As we first walked towards each other at the spot on the Embankment where we'd arranged to meet, a huge gust of wind made a flurry of leaves rain down from the trees, falling around Christopher and making him look like he was in a scene from a film. He threw back his head and laughed.

'I ordered that,' he said, 'and the sunshine!'

He had an infectious smile and we got on immediately. He was no Brad Pitt – actually, he must have taken about 800 pictures of himself before he got the one on his dating profile – but he had a twinkle in his eye and a lovely, soft voice. We sat on the edge of the harbour for a couple of hours, our legs dangling over the side, and felt the unseasonal sun beating down on our backs. We laughed and joked over a couple of glasses of wine, and the conversation flowed freely. I decided that he was a genuinely nice guy, and I didn't resist when he leaned in to kiss me.

Our relationship was like a dream come true. It was a novel experience to have a boyfriend who wasn't completely skint and who washed on a regular basis. Christopher often whisked me off for weekends, if my mum was available to look after Ruby, and we started to spend as much time as possible together, which meant that he was usually at my house if he was not working. I missed him terribly while he was away but I would frequently find the postman knocking on the door to deliver surprise presents from him. It was a fairytale romance and such a contrast to the struggles of the last few years.

Finally, in every way, things seemed to be coming right for me. Life was picture perfect and I was happy to be a good girl at last.

CHAPTER 2

'ARE YOU OK?'

December 2008–September 2009

It's said that when a butterfly flaps its wings it can start a chain of events leading to a hurricane somewhere else in the world. I'm not sure how true that is, or how anyone could even begin to try and prove it, but what I do know is that, sometimes, the smallest, most innocuous action can kick-start a life-changing sequence of events.

It did for me.

As night settled one winter's night, the wood burner in my cottage was blazing. Maxie was sprawled in front of it, his paws twitching as he dreamed of chasing rabbits. Upstairs, Ruby, now four years old, was asleep in her Winnie the Pooh bedroom, her tiny school uniform folded and ready for the next day in Reception class. She'd been tossing and turning for hours that night and I was exhausted. I was living quite a lonely life, the cottage was isolated and I wanted a secure life for Ruby, so I was hesitant about having friends around all the time. Christopher visited sometimes, but I was also wary of bringing anyone into Ruby's life who might not be there for ever. Being a single parent sometimes felt like fighting a losing battle. I loved my little girl dearly, but the demands were relentless and, tonight, just like every evening, I desperately needed to switch off. The difference was, tonight I thought I might actually manage thirty minutes or so to myself. I made a quick cup of coffee and switched my laptop on, planning to answer a few emails and catch up with friends. I was curled up in the armchair with my computer, half watching telly and half looking at other people's posts on Facebook, when a friend request appeared on my screen.

I didn't recognise the name at all and wasn't in the habit of just accepting strangers, so I had a quick look at their profile.

Vic Morana.

The name showed that the link was music-based. I actually had a number of friends in common with Vic and very similar interests, such as festivals and bands. I still adored music and the life I led with Ruby meant that I had to forge links with people where I could, really – if it meant just chatting to them online, so be it, as I wasn't exactly in a position where I could go out to gigs every night. Lucas and I had worked through our differences and were now good friends, and he was consistent about having Ruby every other weekend. I thought Vic might be someone I had met at Glastonbury or a gig – I had a terrible memory for names – so I accepted the request.

That was it.

That was the moment my life changed for ever.

With that one, quick, innocent click, I had let him in.

Looking back on it, it was as if I had opened my front door to a stranger, as if I had thrown away every precaution I'd ever put in place, as if I had freely given access to my whole world – all because of some naïve belief that it was 'just' a friend request on a social media site. The butterfly had flapped its wings and my life would never be the same again.

I had a closer look at his page to see if I could work out how I knew him. Vic was popular, with over 1,300 other Facebook contacts, which was many, many more than I had, but that wasn't surprising as he did seem to be doing really well in his field. I was impressed by everything he had on his page but didn't really expect to have any proper contact with him. I thought I would just see status updates from him every so often, maybe some links to gigs I would be interested in and new music coming out. Nothing happened that night. I chatted to friends, tidied the house a little, and went to bed, thinking that the most noteworthy thing to have occurred was Ruby's sleeping.

Life continued as usual for a couple of weeks and I thought no more about my new 'friend' Vic, but after a while he sent me a message on chat one night, thanking me for accepting his request and saying that he hoped I could support the charity work he was involved in. It wasn't a terribly personal message and it certainly didn't set off any alarm bells. I looked into Vic's page a bit further than I had originally. I learned that he was part of a collective of four DJs, who called themselves StreetBeats. They toured the world doing gigs, and then donated the money they made from their shows back into StreetBeats, which they had set up themselves. The aim was to help street and orphaned kids in Zimbabwe. The charity didn't have any religious or political affiliation, it was just there to help kids who were either existing in shanty towns or who had nowhere to stay and lived rough. Their stories were awful – about 40 per cent lived below the poverty line, and one in ten children didn't go to school. There was a huge problem with sexual exploitation of kids, and trafficking was a growing issue. There were so many other problems. I read that the police were often violent, even to children on the streets, that torture was used by some groups, that minority children faced even more discrimination and abuse. It seemed such a worthy cause. As I thought of Ruby, my heart went out to those other children who had none of the love or privileges she had. We might not be rich, but she would never face a life like that.

The DJs did session work, production, and all sorts of other music-based professional work with well-known singers and bands. It seemed like they really put their hearts into it and raised a great deal of money. Vic was obviously enthusiastic about it. There were no pictures of any of the DJs on the site, and Vic explained that they had a strict rule of no media coverage, saying that they were in the game to raise money for the charity and they weren't interested in any of the 'celebrity' stuff. He was a funny guy and often made me laugh when we were talking online.

He called me 'Miss Henley' a lot and joked about everything and anything. Frequently, awards the collective had won were announced on their Facebook page – MTV awards and things like that – but I respected the way that he didn't play the fame game. When Vic wasn't on tour, he lived in a truck in South Wales. He told me he had Romany gypsy roots and had never lived in a house; it all sounded sublime – I would have loved a life of music and being on the road, but it wasn't likely now that I had responsibilities. He was a bit evasive about some of his family history, but that was fair enough – I was almost a complete stranger to him after all.

Some things best left unsaid, he told me. *Families can be funny things.*

Vic got in touch a few times to tell me more of the work he was doing. One night, I casually mentioned – quite truthfully – that it was a great cause and asked him how he had decided to start it all up. It was as if I'd opened up a flood of memories for him. In previous messages Vic had been chatty and friendly, but it had all been fairly superficial, which was understandable given that we didn't know each other; now, I seemed to have asked the question which went to the very heart of him.

I find this hard to talk about.

Don't say anything – I'm sorry, I replied. *Really, I didn't mean to pry.*

No, you're not prying, he said. *It's just a very raw subject for me.*

It turned out that his whole life and career were based on a heartbreaking accident. Vic's little boy, Zack, had died, run over by a car on a travellers' site when he was less than two years old. Zack's mum was meant to be looking after him, but she was drunk or drugged at the time, according to Vic, and her negligence had cost the poor child his life.

I'll never forgive myself, he said. *She was in charge of him, but I should never have let that happen. I was too busy trying to give her a bit of responsibility and Zack paid the price. She had no interest in keeping him safe, she had no interest in anything apart from what came out of a bottle or went up her nose. I'll regret to my dying day that I didn't put my foot down and say she couldn't have anything to do with my son.*

The site had been on a farm, and the little boy had run out in front of a car – driven by the farmer's wife – so quickly that there was no chance. The poor woman had been driving a 4x4 and hadn't even seen the child. Vic was, naturally, devastated by this and had decided to set up the charity in Zack's memory, to raise money for those street kids in Zimbabwe. He had already sent tens of thousands, keeping nothing for himself or the other members, just focusing on the less fortunate. He told me that StreetBeats had been set up in little Zack's memory and that everyone in the collective just withdrew minimal living expenses, as they are so committed to helping these children.

I tried to reach out to Vic as we chatted online, but it was clear, even through such an impersonal medium, that he was hurting.

This is really painful, Megan – he was just a little boy. I try to block it out but there are times when I get a flash of his tiny body, crumpled and broken, and I can't believe I could have let that happen.

To make matters worse, Vic's relationship with Zack's mum was not good, and he told me she had done everything she could to stand in the way of him being able to see the boy – sadly, Vic hadn't even had much access to him in the months leading up to his death. I told him, *It wasn't your fault! I can tell how much you loved him and it wasn't your choice that she didn't give you access and that you couldn't be there to protect him. It sounds like you were being a really good dad actually – you could have just kept Zack's mum out of the picture entirely but you were trying to keep that link. I'm not with my little girl's father but I do try and make sure he sees her. That's important and it's just heartbreaking that it didn't work out for you.*

Thanks for understanding xxx he replied.

There were a number of Facebook pages for the charity, including Vic's personal page, as well as one called Hippy69, which seemed to be run by everyone involved in the higher echelons of StreetBeats. They had an agent and a pretty punishing schedule, and I knew that their Facebook page was constantly being updated with their location and details of forthcoming tours. They were incredibly popular in Europe and spent a lot of time there, so much that all of the members seemed to constantly be going from one place to another, doing the whole festival and rave circuit, always with their eye on the main reason for their work – to raise money for children living terrible lives in memory of one little boy who had died tragically. Even if Vic wasn't online, someone else from StreetBeats usually was. They worked crazy hours, and I was amazed at their lifestyle – the energy must have kept them going almost twenty-four hours a day, and I felt a bit pathetic that I tended to be exhausted when I was up early with Ruby!

It was as if we crossed a line the night Vic told me about his little boy, and we started to chat much more online. He made me laugh and I needed that sort of easy friendship in my life. I was really touched by his generosity and the way in which he'd managed to make something so good from his own loss. To be honest, it was rare for me to meet people like him and I really admired his strength of character and philanthropy. What did I give him in return? Just a listening ear, really – I wasn't part of his real life, so he could be completely open with me about how much he missed Zack and how much he blamed himself for leaving the child in the care of his unreliable mother. It was a tragedy that Vic really couldn't blame himself for, but I was touched that he had such a strong moral core to even consider that it was all his fault; he was not to blame for the fact that Zack's mother had made it so difficult for him to see his son. The horrific tragedy which followed was due to her choices but Vic didn't see it that way – he blamed himself and was paying the ultimate price, empty and bereft without his son. It was so touching that he would try to make me smile in the middle of his own grief. Every so often, he would say 'Enough about me,' and move on to telling me some silly story. He made me laugh so much. He wasn't flirty, just clever and funny, laid back and chatty. Vic always showed an interest in my life and was really supportive, telling me that being a good parent was the most important thing anyone could do.

He was often abroad with the charity, or in an airport waiting for a flight, which meant that someone else from the collective would check messages on the Street-Beats page and even on his own personal one. He'd be online at the strangest times as his itinerary was mad. Whenever I logged in, he'd be there. I was amazed at the awards they won and the plaudits they got; when he wasn't at gigs or festivals Vic would be working on new mixes, always putting them up online. The gigs were always punted by other people who so enjoyed what he did, and it seemed as if they were in demand across the world. The DJs all trusted each other as they had been through a lot, and Vic seemed particularly close to one member of the group called Valerie. She would reply to me when Vic was unable to, and I started to see her as a friend too, usually chatting through the Hippy69 message option. One day, I got a message from her that made me think that I'd soon be meeting them all.

Hi Megan – just to let you know that we're planning a surprise birthday party for Vic next month. He doesn't have a clue, so PLEASE make sure you don't say anything! I'm trying to get it all organised while he's out of the country. It would be fantastic if you could make it – do you think there's any chance? I've found the perfect place, a barn where we can all have a great time, lots of dancing and music ☺ *I'll send the date and time to you later – fingers crossed that you'll be able to come. I know that he would love to meet you, we all would, so please please do try – and don't mention a word of this to him!*

It sounded fantastic! As soon as Valerie confirmed things, I messaged to say that I would try and get a babysitter and – hopefully – see them there. Over 300 people had accepted the invite and it would be a great party, just what I needed, a night of music and new friends.

I really hope you can, she went on. *Vic has been talking about you so much; I know that he has really enjoyed chatting and says that you've been incredibly understanding about Zack. It was such an awful time for him. He still finds it hard, which is only natural, but he's one of the good guys, he really is, and if we can keep the party secret it'll be fantastic. I just want to see the smile on his face when you walk in! I can't believe he's opened up to you so much already.*

How did she know he's opened up so much? I asked.

Well, he talks about you a lot – and, anyway, we have no secrets, we all share the password for the sites and messages aren't private. You're part of the StreetBeats family now, my dear!

I was really looking forward to the party but there was no ulterior motive. I wasn't attracted to Vic in any way, I hadn't even seen a picture of him, and, although I'd split up with Christopher, I certainly wasn't in the market for another relationship. I just saw Vic as a new friend who had been through a hard time. It was lovely of Valerie to invite me, but I knew that she was asking dozens of others too, lots of them Facebook contacts who only knew Vic through StreetBeats. I did manage to persuade my mum to take Ruby for the night – my parents had divorced by this point, but I tried to keep a good family network for my little girl. Not only did she see her grandparents, but I also made sure Lucas had time with her every other weekend, just as I'd told Vic.

I was all ready to go when, the day before the party, I got another message from Valerie. It was to everyone who had been invited and was to the point.

Sorry, everyone, but the party's been cancelled. Vic's niece has been in a terrible accident and we feel it would be inappropriate for the event to go ahead. We had to tell him it was planned, so he is aware of how much we all care for him. Family comes first though.

That same day, Vic's profile picture changed to one of a cherubic-looking little girl, but there were no posts from him and he wasn't online for days. I messaged Valerie to say that I was thinking of him and was really sorry to hear something bad had happened, but didn't hear back. After a while, I thought I would check with Vic himself to see whether he was OK. I sent a quick message, not prying, not trying to find out any details … just a bit concerned.

Vic got back to me to say that he really appreciated that I got in touch. When he had found out about the planned party, he'd really been looking forward to meeting me.

Any chance of meeting up for coffee? he asked. *I'm not really wanting to be around lots of people yet but I feel I can talk to you. Trust you.*

I said yes, partly because I'd always rather help people out when I can but also partly because Vic lived far enough away from me that, if I didn't want to have any more contact after meeting in real life, there was a decent distance. There was no chance that I would bump into him on the street; I could just gradually fade away online. I only wanted to offer a listening ear while he was having a difficult time; I just hoped that I could offer this kind man some friendly support. Because of the distance, we agreed to meet halfway, in Newbury.

I was already feeling terribly sorry for Vic, but I wasn't entirely relishing meeting up as I wasn't sure I could offer anything, but when I got there he seemed fine and it was very easy. He was clearly a good guy who had suffered a rough life. He started by telling me about how difficult work was – the management who controlled them as DJs were just pushing them into the most horrendous schedule. I knew that already as I'd seen how hard he worked by watching stuff online, but he then went on to tell me things I could never have imagined.

'Life's been hard,' he said, and it was such an understatement. He told me so much about his abusive childhood and various losses, and I was really touched that he felt safe enough to reveal all of this. He was, after all, a superstar DJ and yet he was so alone; I also felt very privileged that someone like him trusted someone like me.

Vic's story was a dramatic and complicated one. He touched again on the loss of Zack, but it transpired that there were troubles running through the whole Morana family. I listened for ages as he told me of the recent death of his niece, of his Romany background, and of the threats he kept getting as he tried to break out of the culture that kept reeling him back in. Vic was shaking as he told me his story, and said that he never imagined he would be able to tell one person so much in such a short time.

'I'd just like a quiet life, but there's not much chance with my family,' he revealed. 'I've got to go to Dina's funeral next week.'

'Funerals are never easy,' I agreed.

'No, no, that's true, but this one …' he began.

'Well, she was so young,' I said. It was all I knew really, that she was ten years old.

'More than that … God!' he exclaimed, putting his hands to his face and rubbing his eyes. 'Megan – my family. I don't know where to start.'

'You don't have to tell me anything,' I assured him.

'But I want to – I feel like I can talk to you. You see, I don't really have anyone. Leah, Valerie, Clare – they're all brilliant, brilliant DJs, brilliant people, but the management company has us over a barrel so I hardly ever see them. They're a lifeline but they have their own careers and their own lives.' He laughed bitterly. 'You're about the only real person I've spoken to in real life that I can trust for months.'

His story came pouring out.

'Kat, my sister, is a bloody nightmare. Of course it's heartbreaking that she's lost her kid, no one knows how that feels more than I do, but … she was a shit mother. She'd go off for days on end, leaving Dina by herself. You'd think she would have changed by now, but she only cares for herself – now her daughter's paid the price.'

It transpired that Kat owned a yard in Manchester and she rented out spaces in it to other gypsies. She'd leave for days on end, paying a couple of hundred quid to people she barely knew to look out for her child.

They rarely did. Dina had got out of the yard, and had virtually run out in front of a car. He had been really close to Dina, as his sister was a terrible mother from the outset from what I could gather, and frequently left her daughter for long periods of time while she went off sorting out drug deals and other dodgy stuff. Kat was still heavily involved in the Romany culture they had been born into. She was really violent and very rich due to her drug dealing. Their father, Jay, sounded like a real nasty piece of work; from what I could tell he was some kind of gypsy king who kept lots of people in fear and at his beck and call. Vic's mother and father lived in Spain and it sounded like Kat was determined to follow in their footsteps. Vic would often bring Dina to stay with him whenever he was back in England, and had been trying to negotiate with his sister for the child to come and live with him as she was so neglected by her mother. He told me that Dina regarded him as her father figure and he, in turn, desperately missed having a child of his own.

'It just brings everything back that I went through with Zack,' Vic said quietly. 'I can't believe another little one has been lost.'

It was awful – but what was really getting to Vic was that, by going to the funeral, he would be right back in the middle of the family he had tried to escape many years ago. Vic had been living as a New Age traveller for the past fifteen years, a break from how he was raised, but it was as if they keep reeling him back in. His parents had moved back to Spain when he was in his twenties and he was now forty-one. Kat had never tried to leave the gypsy community. In fact, it sounded as if she revelled in the drama and violence. She sounded like a bit of a thug herself, acting as her father's minion and glorying in the punishments meted out to anyone who crossed them.

'She's completely unhinged,' Vic told me. 'Unpredictable, vengeful – I wonder how we can be related at all sometimes. Of course, I'd do anything to protect the people I love, but Kat jumps in so soon; it only takes a look her way for her to decide someone needs sorting. If anyone pisses her off, she's after them. And she would decide you'd pissed her off as soon as look at you.'

She sounded awful; only a few years younger than Vic, but already embroiled in a life of drugs and violence. The way she had neglected Dina didn't appear to have had any impact on her, and no one but Vic was blaming her. She seemed to be the golden girl of the family as she just followed their path, whereas Vic was the outsider, and he was hated for breaking free.

'It's such a relief to get this off my chest; I feel as if I've known you for ever,' he told me. 'It's so odd – I just get this sense that we've got a connection; no one else seems to "get" me in this same way. I can't believe we've only just met.' I knew what he meant. I felt as if I'd made an immediate, true friend.

It was lovely that we had shared so much that day but I wasn't sure that I'd ever see him in person again; maybe the odd FB message, but I was convinced it would fizzle out. He had struck me as a bit of a paradox – needy and tragic on one hand, but he was also this superstar DJ with his MTV awards and lauded public appearances. Two sides of one personality – both of which were quite attractive. I wanted to protect him, to be honest, but he was so cool and successful that he was out of my league. He knew so many people: he had DJ'd at Fatboy Slim's fortieth birthday party, done tracks with the Prodigy, he'd gone out with Katie Melua for a while, been sought after by the best drum and bass people. He'd been on the scene for so long that he knew everyone and was known by them all. He'd seen people come and go, and was still recovering from the loss of good friends who hadn't been as strong as him and had succumbed to drink or drugs or just the lure of an unsustainable lifestyle. Amy Winehouse was a good friend of his, and he spoke of her with such affection, telling me he hated the way her talent was being wasted when she could have such amazing things ahead of her if someone would only step in and set her on the right path. They both spent hours talking about their tattoos, what they planned to get next, and who the best artists were. Vic stayed out of the drug scene and only really drank socially, but he could see the damage it did to others. He really did mix in an amazing world.

'With my family, it's best to keep on your toes,' he told me. 'It's best to not get involved in anything that can dull your senses. You never know who's watching, who's behind you.'

It was incredible that he was such a success, given all he had to think about. It would have been easy for him to just slide into a life of threats and violence, to take his place in the gypsy hierarchy, but I found him inspirational in the way he had made his own way and rejected all of that.

When we finally parted company, we hugged, and I was glad that Vic had been able to confide in me. No one should have to face his challenges alone, and the more people he had on his side, the better. I was so glad to have had the chance to meet him, but, to be honest, had no plans to meet again. I was used to picking up 'waifs and strays', but I'd never expected that it would be something that would cause me such hurt; and I certainly had no idea that, this time, a trap had been set.

CHAPTER 3

FRIENDS

September 2009–November 2009

I didn't know whether telling me such upsetting things had distressed Vic more than he let on, but within days of our meeting he posted that he was going to stop work for a while to deal with 'personal stuff'. Street-Beats would be kept going by Valerie, and the two other members of the collective he'd spoken about, Leah and Clare. I was soon getting messages from all three, who were always friendly and chatty, although clearly worried about Vic.

In one of her first comments to me, Leah said:

We all so glad he met you Megan. He not stopped talking about you and how he felt he could tell you anything. For Vic to have that sort of instant connection with anyone is so special – he a friendly guy, but quite guarded given his background. You good for him!

It turned out that Leah was Belgian, so her English was sometimes a little erratic, but a million times better than my attempts at any other language! Clare agreed with what her colleague and friend had said:

Vic's having hard time but u have made it so much better. When he came back from meeting u he had obviously got so much out of his system. Think that's where he got strength to take a bit of time out. Thanks hun xx

They all told me that meeting me had been the only positive thing to happen to Vic in a long while. I didn't feel overwhelmed by them, they were all so nice, but I do admit to being flattered. I'd broken up with Christopher and sworn off men for a very long time – possibly for ever, given how I felt – but this was all innocent and playful. Valerie had previously told me how there were always groupies hanging around gigs, and that women were constantly throwing themselves at Vic. She also said that he had no interest in that sort of encounter and that it would have to be a very special person who caught his heart. I didn't think for a minute that was me, I wasn't attracted to him in that way at all, but it was nice to think that someone so successful, so sought after, had seen something in me that was different.

Valerie was by far the chattiest of the collective members and she was the one I'd been in contact with almost from the start. She started to tell me much more about Vic's life and confirmed so much of what he had told me; in fact, from what she said, he'd actually held back on a lot of things. Vic's father, Jay, had been terribly abusive, throwing him into baths of boiling hot water as a child, scrubbing him with abrasive kitchen cleaner, beating him senseless. Vic had been around guns and knives since he was a baby, even putting a gun in his own mouth when he was four. His dad had been arrested for murder at one point, but got off through some sort of bribe that his cohorts had managed to set up. All of this affected me a great deal. Ruby was still so little and anything to do with cruelty to children broke my heart – first the charity, now this. I could barely believe the awfulness of some parents, as Vic's mother, Isabella, had colluded with so much of the violence and abuse. From what he had told me, she was too scared of Jay herself to stand up to him and stop him hurting the kids, but I just couldn't understand what kind of mother would stay in that situation. Although his mother was afraid of his father, she was always kind to the kids, and would cuddle the children and tend to their injuries whenever he was out of sight. Vic had a lot of love for his mother and never blamed her for not standing up to his dad as he realised what an impossible predicament she was in. The gypsy situation was certainly baffling. For Vic to have come through all of that and then lose his own son seemed a terrible tragedy.

Valerie was never over the top in what she told me – there was a balance between talking about music and telling me how he was amazing to have come through so much, and I couldn't help agreeing. I genuinely felt that he was one of the good guys. Some people let their pasts consume them, but Vic was so keen to help others and make a new life for himself. With Valerie, Leah and Clare all telling me that he was smitten, I suppose I wasn't entirely surprised when, one day, unannounced, Vic turned up at my house.

'Guess who?' he said, with a sheepish grin when I opened the door. 'Was just passing, so thought I'd give you the pleasure of my company for a little while, Miss Henley.'

'Just passing more than two hundred miles or so?' I asked. 'That sounds plausible!'

I invited him in for a coffee and we chatted just as easily as we had the first time.

'I'm really sorry that things have been so hard for you,' I told him. We were sitting in my kitchen, with the sun streaming in gloriously, big mugs of tea in our hands, and Maxie desperately trying to get some attention from the visitor. He didn't have to try very hard; Vic cuddled and played with him, and I could see that he loved dogs. I felt very comfortable with Vic, especially given how good he was with Maxie, but wasn't too sure why he was here. 'Are you back at work yet?'

'Now and again, bits and bobs,' he answered distractedly. 'Nice dog.'

The way he was with Maxie was one of the things I really liked about Vic. I always thought – and still do – that you can tell a lot about a person by how they are with animals. He didn't fuss, he didn't go overboard; he was just natural and friendly with my dog. We had a lovely time for a couple of hours or so, talking about everything and nothing. It felt very relaxed but I really needed to get to work.

'No problem,' he said. 'I just wanted to see you really, Miss Henley. You cheer me up, you do.'

I had to smile. The way he called me 'Miss Henley' was sweet. I knew that he wasn't being formal, but it felt warm, not too pushy, not as if he was making a pet name for me, just a little in-joke between new friends.

'Just need to pop to the loo, then I'll be heading off,' I told him.

Vic swept his arm before him in a grand gesture.

'Whatever the lady needs to do,' he said. 'I'll wait here and see you off the premises.'

I heard him rinsing the cups as I ran upstairs. Five minutes later, I was ready to go. He held the kitchen door for me and I locked it behind us. Walking over to my car, he waited while I put the key in the ignition.

'Have a successful novelty-buying trip,' he winked, referring to my appointment at an old country house, where I was hoping to pick up some things for my business.

'I'll do what I can,' I told him, turning the key.

Nothing.

The engine tried to turn over, but nothing.

I tried again, with the same result.

'Bugger,' I muttered.

Vic had been walking back to his own car, but turned back. 'Problem?' he asked.

'Not sure why it's being temperamental now,' I sighed, trying it again. 'It's usually no bother.'

Still, there was no sign of life.

'Really?' I hissed.

'I don't know much about cars,' said Vic quietly, screwing up his eyes and looking at it hopelessly. 'Any ideas?'

'Absolutely none …' I admitted. 'Maybe I should just leave it a minute and try again?'

'Can't do any harm,' he agreed.

He got in the car and waited beside me, both of us useless, and then I tried again. And again. And again. Completely dead.

'Oh, God!' I wailed, thumping the steering wheel. 'I've got to get to that appointment, and pick Ruby up, and a hundred other things! I'll have to see if I can get a garage to come out and collect it. It's always been such a reliable car – why now?' I said, knowing full well that I didn't have the money for a garage to come to the house, but not seeing what else I could do.

'Take mine,' said Vic.

'What?'

'Take my car – go to your appointment, load the boot up with what you buy, get your little girl, and I'll help you unload it all when you get back.'

'Really? Are you sure? You're a lifesaver!' I declared, kissing him on the cheek. 'Do you not need to be anywhere?'

He looked at me, the sadness welling up in his eyes. 'To be honest, Megan, I'd rather not be around anyone just now. You calm me down, you don't expect anything from me. I'll wait here, have a little think with your lovely dog at my side, and the tea will be brewed when you get back.'

I was so relieved. He maybe didn't know anything about cars, but Vic had made my day a whole lot easier with that one offer. By the time I got back – with Ruby and a pile of treasure – there was a pot of tea and dinner waiting on me, Max had been walked and I had a vague feeling that some tidying up had been attempted.

'Just call me your guardian angel,' smiled Vic. By the time Ruby was in bed, we'd come to an agreement. He would kindly let me use his car for as long as I needed it in exchange for being able to sleep on the sofa and get some peace.

'I love everyone in the collective,' he told me as the day drew to a close, 'but, by God, do I need a break from the sympathetic looks and sad faces. You, Miss Henley, treat me as if I'm almost normal.'

He was a perfect gentlemen. There was nothing physical between us, he never pushed his luck in any way; we just muddled along for a couple of days exchanging my sofa for his car. I knew that he needed to get his head together after all of the troubles he'd been through, and, to be honest, it was nice to have him around. He seemed safe – and I needed that. There was also a part of me which enjoyed being able to provide a refuge for such a damaged soul; I wasn't sexually attracted to Vic in the slightest but I did want to be there for him, to be supportive and kind. I also liked the fact that he usually lived four hours away, so if things did go sour it wasn't as if he would be able to keep popping in. He was a thoughtful house guest, always willing to take Max for a walk or help Lily with her homework, and on the fourth day he also suggested that he give me a hand while I looked for a new car.

'I can't fix them,' he said, 'but I can hopefully stop you getting sold an old banger again.'

I jumped at the chance. A couple of days later we found the perfect one for me – it was cheap (it had to be), but it seemed in great condition. Vic helped me to get a good deal, and I drove home elated.

'That's you sorted then,' he told me that night, 'and I feel a million times better too. I can't thank you enough for giving me this time to just be here without any demands.' He said he'd be leaving the next day around lunchtime, and we made plans to meet up at the start of the next month.

I drove Ruby to school and got home just in time to find Vic loading up his own car. He didn't have much luggage as he hadn't planned to stay to begin with, so it wouldn't take long. 'Is there anything else you need for the trip?' I asked him.

'A sandwich?' he asked, trying to give me puppy dog eyes. 'Some biscuits?'

I laughed. 'Go on then – I'll do you a packed lunch if you give me a couple of minutes!' However, as I was getting things ready it dawned on me how nice it had been to have him around. He must have been thinking the same thing because, as I absentmindedly buttered the bread, he wandered into the kitchen.

'Megan …' he began, 'I don't want you to feel under any pressure at all but …'

'I know exactly what you're going to say,' I told him.

'Are you a mind reader, Miss Henley?' he asked, laughing.

'I can certainly tell when someone is easy and there's no need to change it,' I replied.

'So – I'll unpack the car, will I?' he asked, giving me a hug. I nodded and hugged him back.

We were very comfortable around each other and, one night, when I was in the living room listing stock on my website, Vic came in.

'Megan,' he began. 'I'm not sure how to say this but … I've just had a really odd email.'

He'd been lazing around in the kitchen on his own laptop when the first message had come through.

Having fun with your slag?

'Do they mean me?' I screeched. 'Who sent that?'

He shrugged. 'I have no idea. I mean, I assume it's talking about you, but it doesn't say who it's from.'

'Well, who have you been talking to? Who does it say it's from?'

'See for yourself,' he replied.

The email address it was from simply read 'a friend', then the host. I was no expert on anything technological.

'You must be able to find out who it's from?'

'I'm as clueless as you. Only the collective know about you, really, and it obviously isn't from them. But Megan – it isn't the only one.'

He showed me a series of emails that had come in, with about ten minutes between each one.

She's a liar you know.

You needn't think she'll make you happy.

She'll lie to you, cheat on you, play you for a fool.

Have you worked out that she's a dirty whore yet?

You must be an idiot to be hanging around that slut.

'Vic! These are absolutely horrible – what can we do? Call the police?' I said.

'Not likely,' he scoffed. 'No one's saying stuff like that about you, no one.' Vic held out his arms to me and I buried my head in his chest. Who hated me so much that they would say these things?

'It must be someone you know,' I told him. 'If they were sent to your email address, they must know you and they're being nasty to you.'

He thought for a bit. 'Maybe. It's easy enough to find a way to email me, but it's a bit odd that they've picked on you rather than just tell me that I'm a tosser or something like that. It's … well, it's a bit personal to you, really.'

He was right. It was horrible to have these things, these lies, said about me by someone I didn't know. The tears started falling uncontrollably as Vic tried to console me.

'It's all a lot of crap,' he said. 'Someone just doesn't want us to be happy – and, do you know what, Miss Henley? I've been very happy indeed here with you since your rubbish car managed to bring us together.'

He turned my face up towards his and kissed me properly for the first time. We'd mucked about a bit before, sometimes play-fighting and tickling each other like overgrown kids, but, this time, we finally admitted just how close we'd grown. Something horrible had brought us together, but now we had eventually broken down the barriers and shown how we felt about each other.

We stayed on the sofa that evening, wrapped up in each other, and I finally calmed down. The next morning, Vic was up and about before I woke. When I rubbed my eyes and stretched my legs, there was a cup of tea beside me and he was making a cushion pile for Maxie on the floor beside me.

'Well, it looks like he'll be comfortable,' I smiled.

'Got to keep the boss of the house happy, haven't we?' said Vic.

'Is that me or Maxie?' I asked.

'You'll never know,' he laughed, as Maxie settled happily into his new sleep area. 'Ruby's had her breakfast and she's getting ready for school. I'll drop her off – you just take your time to face the day, my love.'

He was so kind, so genuine. He was funny and played well with Ruby. I loved that he didn't mind making a fool of himself with her when they played; that was a good sign in my mind. There was never any pressure from him for me to do anything or to say anything; it was all at my pace, and I felt so lucky to have him around. I dreaded to think how I would have coped without him, given all of my car problems, and I now felt rotten that I was bringing all of this trouble to his door with the nasty emails. Hopefully, that was a one-off; whoever had sent them had got their cheap thrill, and it had backfired in any case. Instead of the lies making Vic doubt me, it had brought us much closer together.

With Ruby at school, and Max ensconced for the day, Vic and I pottered about in the cottage for the rest of the morning. He would kiss me on the cheek or the top of my head every time he passed, but I didn't feel his affection was claustrophobic in any way.

While I was in the kitchen making us some lunch, I heard him call to me.

'Megan? Megan, love – can you come here for a minute?'

He was sitting at his laptop and my heart sank. I just knew, from the look on his face, that there had been more messages. I was right.

Are you stupid?

Why are you digging yourself in deeper?

You know she's a liar, I told you that.

Do you know she's a prostitute too?

Do you know she has sex with any man who will pay her?

Do you have any idea how many men she has slept with?

Has she told you? She won't have told you. She's a liar and a slag.

Ask her. Ask her what it's like being a whore. Ask her.

The same comments, over and over again. Whoever it was just kept on sending message after message. Vic's inbox was full of them – all from 'a friend'.

Liar.

Whore.

Slag.

Prostitute.

Liar.

Whore.

Slag.

Prostitute.

Liar.

Whore.

Slag.

Prostitute.

I sat there, beside Vic, and couldn't believe the quantity of the messages. Why was someone doing this? Who was doing this? Why were they sending them to Vic? Did that mean they hated me or him?

It went on for the next three days, non-stop. Every time Vic looked, there were more messages. Again I suggested calling the police, but he told me that he was giving 'a friend' enough rope to hang themselves. I had to ask him the question that was tearing me up.

'Vic – do you believe them?' I whispered.

He looked at me with horror.

'How can you even ask that?' he replied. 'It's maybe a bit early to say this, but I adore you, Miss Henley. This nasty piece of work hasn't accounted for that. There's only one liar here, and that's them.' I was so relieved, but I still didn't know why it was happening. 'I don't know,' admitted Vic. 'Jealousy? Jealous of me; jealous of us? People can be nasty …'

He'd been through so much already; I hated the thought that I was the person who was bringing even more trouble to his door, but Vic assured me that all he cared about was how this was affecting me. That night, however, the nastiness got even worse. It was as if the person calling themselves 'a friend' was just pushing and pushing in the hope that they would finally get a reaction.

Have you found the pictures yet? they asked.

Have you found the special photographs your girlfriend likes posing for?

'What are they talking about?' asked Vic.

'I've no idea! It's just another lie,' I told him.

Does she not make enough money being a prostitute?

Does she make more money from doing porn or more from having sex with strangers?

Do you think you'll catch something, Vic?

Are you worried that your girlfriend is such a slag?

Do you think your friends will see her porn pics?

Do you hate her for posing like that?

53

Do you hate her for being a whore?
Do you hate her, Vic?

It was non-stop and, after the first couple of days, started to flood in from a lot of different sources and different email addresses. 'A friend' was joined by 'Friend 101', 'Another Friend', 'Justlookingoutforyou', and dozens more. It was as if Vic was getting hardly any other correspondence, just a deluge of this nasty stuff from God knows where.

'I've had enough of this,' he told me. 'You just get on with your life, look after Ruby, look after Maxie. I'll deal with this. I'll find out who has done this, don't you worry.'

But Vic was as useless with computers as I was. There was no way either of us could tackle this on our own. I was so ashamed at what was being said about me, but Vic needed to contact a friend of his called Martin, who was a computer expert. They'd lost touch with each other in the past few years, so I agreed that Vic could tell Valerie what was going on in the hope that she could find the man who might be able to help us.

Don't you worry, darling, she messaged, *Vic's great to have on your side when things go wrong but God help anyone who messes with him or those he cares for. He'll sort this out, don't doubt that. With a family like his, he's learned plenty in the past about tracking people down and fixing them.*

He couldn't do it alone, but, thankfully, Valerie did find Martin. He was living in Spain, but more than happy to help us out. My relief at his offer of assistance was soon overcome by the horror of what he found.

Vic/Megan – who is Christopher? he emailed one day.

Christopher.

My ex.

From that point, with Martin's help, it all became clear. At some point – while we were together, or just as we split up – Christopher had placed some very sophisticated spyware on my laptop. He had been able to read all of my emails and FB messages, knew everything I had said to Vic, Valerie and the others, and was well aware that I was falling into a relationship with another man. Martin managed to remove the spyware and put a lot of complicated protection in place, but he also warned me that there was no way of knowing how long Christopher had been spying on me. I felt so vulnerable. I'd been going about my business, messaging and emailing, and all the time I was being watched. I had trusted Christopher, I'd had a relationship with him, and yet this was what he really thought of me.

Vic had been sent such disgusting messages – and now I felt that they showed what Christopher really thought of me. I was so grateful to Vic for his help, but I did feel exposed in front of him. He didn't know me well enough to really appreciate that Christopher's words were all lies; for all he knew, I could have been some porn-loving, lying prostitute.

There was stress in every area of my life by now – broken cars, people telling lies about me, discovering that I'd been spied on for goodness knows how long. Thank God there was someone to look out for me. Vic continued to care, he continued to indulge Max, and be great with Ruby. He didn't bombard me with gushing declarations of love, but he surrounded me with safety and security. He was a sweet, caring guy – maybe he wouldn't win any beauty awards, but that isn't what matters. I thought he had an amazing strength of character to have recovered from so much and yet still be trying to make other people's lives better, and now going out of his way to help me. He was strong, he was emotionally connected – he was just what I needed, and I don't believe life is a rehearsal … so I fell for him.

Hook, line and sinker.

CHAPTER 4

MAD

November 2009

I was actually really scared of what Christopher might do. During our relationship, he had shown some possessive tendencies, but this was beyond anything I'd thought he was capable of – I was terrified he might turn up at the door, so having Vic there was a relief. Our relationship had progressed quite quickly, I guess, but it was based on him being so kind and helpful to me. Most men would have run a mile if they'd been sent the sort of emails he'd been receiving, especially when they worked out it was their new girlfriend's ex using spyware and all sorts of weird stuff. His caring side made me feel so safe, and I was starting to see that he had a front for the rest of the world that I was privileged to see behind.

I knew that Vic had his own issues to work through with the losses of Zack and Dina, but I hoped I could help him find a happier life. However, in early

November I discovered just how trying things were for him.

All of a sudden he, quite literally, went mad.

Vic had been open with me about the fact that he had suffered from some mental health problems in the past. I was completely supportive, feeling that it was certainly nothing to be ashamed of and glad that he could trust me. I knew that he had been severely depressed after the death of Zack and that, when Dina was killed, many of those feelings came back again. It was perfectly natural really. He also had enormous feelings of guilt, which had an effect on his mental health. Although his family was nasty and violent, they were still his blood. It must be so hard to break away from your mother and father and sister, even when they are toxic. Vic had alluded to past events when he had first made it clear to them that he would take no part in their lifestyle – he had then been threatened and harassed, which had made his mental health even more fragile. All of this seemed perfectly understandable to me; I also had friends who suffered from depression, and other issues, and I knew that the last thing they needed was for anyone to be judgemental or intrusive, so I didn't push Vic for details, I just let him speak about it whenever he chose to.

What he hadn't told me was that things could get a whole lot worse than a bout of depression. When I say that, I don't mean to minimise depression in any way. I know it's horrible, I know it can be completely debilitating, but I also know that many, many people live with it and manage it. I could support that and I could help Vic with it, but I had no experience of the terrors he was really going through.

One day, when I was working in the spare room, organising my stock and getting ready for an upcoming vintage fair, I heard a scream coming from the living room where I knew Vic was.

'Noooooooooooooooooo!'

As I ran to him, thinking he'd had an accident, I heard it again.

'Noooooooooooooooooo! Please stop! Please stop!'

It almost didn't sound like Vic, it sounded like a child.

When I got there, he was crouched in a corner with his arms around him, rocking back and forth, in tears.

'Vic! What's wrong?' I asked, in a panic. 'Have you hurt yourself?'

He looked up at me as if he'd never seen me before.

'Who are you?' he asked, in a whisper. 'Are you going to help me? Are you going to hurt me? Did Nice Lady send you? Or him? Did Skill send you?'

I was shocked. The poor man looked terrified and he had the voice of a five-year-old.

'Vic, it's me, Megan – what's happened?'

'Megan?' he said questioningly, as if it was a name he was hearing for the first time. 'Megan?'

'Yes, Megan – what's going on, Vic?'

'Tell the Bad Man to stop, please,' he said softly. 'Tell the Bad Man to stop telling me these things, I don't want to hurt myself. Ask him to stop telling me to hurt myself please, Megan.'

'What bad man?' I asked. 'There's no one here except us.'

'THERE IS A BAD MAN!' he shouted. 'Can't you hear him? Can't you hear them all? I'm scared, Megan. Are you scared?'

'No, I'm not scared because there's no one else here, Vic …' I began.

'YOU SHOULD BE SCARED!' he shouted. 'They want me to hurt YOU too. Hurt me, hurt you. Hurt me, hurt you. Hurt Vic, hurt Megan. Hurt me, hurt you,' he said, in a singsong voice, still rocking, still holding himself tightly. 'I don't want to do it, I don't want to do those things. Why do they want me to be bad? I'm not bad, I don't want to hurt myself, please don't let me hurt you, Megan. Please don't let them make me, please!'

This went on for ages. He was convinced there were other people – I don't know how many, but there was definitely one he referred to as the Bad Man and also a Nice Lady and one called Skill – and that they wanted him to do bad things to himself and to me. He looked awful, almost like someone in a film, going through such mental terrors. It was dreadful to watch and I felt completely powerless. I had absolutely no experience with anything like this and all I could do was sit on guard to make sure that Vic didn't harm himself in any way. I found myself scanning the room to see if there was anything sharp, anything at all that he might be able to use to cut himself, as he was obviously still hearing things in his head and I didn't want him to rush for a weapon and do something awful.

After a while, he seemed to calm down a bit and he stopped talking so much about 'them'. 'Vic,' I said, quietly, 'we need to get you to someone who can help. Is that OK?'

'No one can help,' he moaned. 'This has been going on for years. No one can help, I just have to live with it. It'll go – but it'll come back again too.' By this time, he had come out of the corner and was lying in my arms on the sofa. 'I've tried. No one can help. I'm scared, Megan. I've always been scared that they'll win, that one day I'll hurt myself, but now it's worse.'

'Why?' I asked. 'Why is it worse now?'

He pulled away from me and stared into my eyes.

'Don't you see? They want me to hurt you. Maybe I will. Maybe I'll hurt you, Megan. Maybe I'll do something really awful to you and I won't be able to help myself because it won't really be me, will it?'

This, naturally, terrified me. I had absolutely no experience of dealing with someone with this level of mental distress, and I needed help. As all of this was going through my mind, Vic was still talking.

'It's been going on for years, years and years and years. I can barely sleep at night, that's when it gets worse. You've made it better, you've made things so much calmer, but they're getting stronger again. The Bad Man is angry that you've got such control and that's why he wants me to hurt you. He says that if I get rid of you, we'll all be better off. Skill says it would be quick – I could hurt you quickly, then it would be better, just me and him and the others. But … he says I could take my time hurting you if I want to as well.'

I had no idea what to say. The man I was falling in love with was telling me that he might kill me because of voices in his head. If I was lucky, it might be quick – but he might draw it out if he felt that way when the time came. How could I even begin to process that?

'I know that I walk about some nights, that I go wandering – sometimes I have to go do what they tell me to do, but I'll try, Megan, I'll try so hard to keep you safe. Please believe me.'

'We have to get you to a doctor, Vic,' I said. 'They can help with this.'

He shook his head. 'They really can't. This is something I just have to deal with. You have no idea what my childhood was like, the abuse, the horrors. I've been alone for so long – until I found you, there was no one to share anything with. Friends, people I work with, they're nothing compared to you, but you can't change what's been done to me. My father used to glory in being vile to me. He abused me in every way you can think of, I swear he must have spent hours thinking of new ways to make me wish I was dead. He's an awful man, Megan. My sister Kat has a daughter called Willow. Dad arranged for Willow to be raped when she was fourteen. He actually paid someone to do it to keep control.'

'He paid for someone to rape his own grandchild?' I asked incredulously.

'Yes, he wanted to keep her in her place and show Kat that he was in charge, no matter what. What he says goes, always – and he'll use any means possible to ensure everyone around him knows that. He's always got his own way. When anyone tries to stand up to him, they regret it.'

'But you got out,' I reminded him.

'And he often makes me regret it,' Vic whispered, almost to himself.

'Have you never had any help for any of this?'

He laughed. 'How could I? We never stayed in the one place for any length of time. No one in authority was trusted – and doctors came into that category. I couldn't be honest with my parents about how their treatment of me was making my brain go mad – they'd have tried to beat it out of me, and there was hardly an inch of me that wasn't battered and bruised as it was. There were no teachers and everyone we knew in the community was scared of my father. He's the Gypsy King, the head guy – if his kid told someone what I could have told them, they wouldn't have seen the next day. I kept it to myself; we never saw doctors, never trusted anyone, and then, when I was older and got away, well, that mentality stays with you. I find it very hard to trust anyone, Megan – you have no idea how much I've changed around you.'

I felt so bad for him. I felt incredibly selfish, for thinking only about how I might be in danger (which wasn't that likely given that he obviously cared for me so much and was fighting his demons), while he had been battling since he was just a little kid.

'Let's go to my GP, Vic,' I suggested again. 'I'm with you now, I can help.'

'No GP will even look at me!' he said. 'You need to know this – my lifestyle, the way my people exist … they don't even register a baby's birth. They don't want to be on a list somewhere, be noticed by those in charge. Kids don't go to school, they avoid hospitals whenever they can. They want to stay off the radar. If anyone knows a child has been born, they get involved, and that's the last thing the gypsies want.'

'What are you saying, Vic? Was your birth never registered?'

He laughed bitterly. 'I'm nothing, Megan. I don't exist.'

It was chilling.

I still wanted him to see a doctor but, given all of this, how could that happen?

'Maybe we could say you're a friend visiting from abroad?' I suggested. As I said it, another thought popped into my mind. 'Vic – how do you travel?'

'What?' he asked.

'With StreetBeats and holidays and everything – how do you travel? If you've never officially existed, how can you travel without a passport.'

He stared at me intently.

'Megan, Megan, Megan,' he said, stroking my cheek. 'Do you have any idea what a breath of fresh air you are? To have someone like you in my life, so innocent, so untarnished by all of this ... you could save me, you could.'

He kissed me gently.

At that moment I wanted to save him, I really did.

'I have a passport. It just isn't me.'

'What do you mean?'

'Well, when I turned eighteen I tried to get one for the first time. I hadn't really thought it through, but I wanted to travel, so it was the next logical step. That's when I was told the truth – there was no record of me, Megan. I was nothing. But, there were people who could help me. Some others in the gypsy community got me a false identity of a guy who had died. Officially, online, in records, I'm Steven Cook. He's six years older than me, but, for anything that needs a paper trail, that's who I am.'

Given what he'd told me about how the gypsy community worked, that made sense – they would be able to access dodgy passports and fake identity documents, and it would be a way of keeping themselves off the grid. His life had been so hard and he wasn't even getting any peace in his life now.

'Vic,' I told him, 'I'll do everything I can to help you – but you have to accept that help.'

'I'm a proud man, Megan …'

'I know, but I want to be there for you just as you've been there for me. I want to do everything I can to help you get your life on an even keel. Will you please let me? Please?'

He sighed and put his head on my shoulder.

'What have I done to deserve you, Miss Henley?' he whispered.

Vic dozed for a little while as I called my GP practice. They said to bring him in as soon as possible, but when I went to tell him he had gone. I called his name and checked every room, before finally finding him in the basement. His demons were back – he was sitting straight up on a chair, with wild eyes and a crazed look. He was a different person. He seemed terrified, frozen and little, so altered from the funny, confident man I had fallen for. I had never seen anyone with that sort of expression on their face. He looked tortured.

'He wants me to find a high building. He wants me to jump off.'

'Who does, Vic? Who do you think is talking to you this time?' I asked.

'Skill, he's called Skill, that's his name.'

'Have you heard him before?'

He nodded.

'For a long time?'

He nodded again.

'Since I was little … five of them. Nice Lady … she tries to help, but Skill … I've to find a high building Megan, I've to jump.'

He cocked his head to the side as if listening.

'A river, he wants me to find a river and not swim. I've to drown myself, Megan. Skill says it's for the best.'

The voices were torturing him. He genuinely seemed to be hearing things. He showed me his hands – they were covered in scars, which I'd obviously seen before, but now he told me that Skill and another man he heard had told him to cut himself. The other voice was called Red Man and he was just as nasty as Skill, just as damaging to Vic. His whole persona had changed dramatically and my heart was breaking for him.

I bundled him into my car – he was still shaking and whispering to himself – and headed for the medical centre. I quickly explained to the doctor what was going on and she made an instant decision.

'Wait here, I'll make a phone call.'

Within seconds, she was back. Vic had spent the short time looking around with a look of panic in his eyes as if he recognised nothing. Different expressions kept flitting across his face as if one of the voices had said something, but he didn't share their comments with me. It looked as if he was being tortured from inside.

'Megan's going to take you to the Woodlands Clinic, OK, Vic? They're all very nice there, it's a bit like a hotel,' the doctor said.

'No, no, no,' Vic started to moan.

'It'll be fine,' I said, trying to comfort him. 'Really, I won't leave you; I'll make sure you're safe. I'll stay with you the whole time.'

'I don't want to go there, Megan!'

'I know, I know,' I soothed. 'They can help you, though – they can help you feel better, then you can get back to being yourself. Won't that be good?'

He looked at me as if I had his life in my hands. I drove to the clinic, parked and went into the reception with Vic holding my hand. On the right was a little room we were shown into – you could see through the glass door into the main hospital and we could see the in-patients. It was such a cliché. There were people just walking around, looking mad to be honest, some of them drugged, some of them terrifying-looking, some of them confused. It was a very strange experience for me, but Vic seemed detached from it.

In the room were two members of staff from the Crisis Team. 'We need to admit him immediately,' said the first member of the team, speaking to me as if Vic wasn't there. 'He seems in quite a bad way and the best way to deal with that is to have him here, residentially.'

The other team member was being saccharin sweet to him, talking patronisingly as if he was three years old, or a bit simple in the head. 'Wouldn't that be nice, Vic? You could just come in here for a little while and not have any worries. Oh, I'd quite like that myself! Just pop in, let us take care of everything, and then, hopefully, everything will be all sorted very soon indeed.'

Vic wouldn't engage at all. He was curled up in a ball with his face hidden. He didn't say a word for so long.

'We think it's best that you stay here for a little while,' said the sickeningly sweet one. 'Is that OK with you? Did you hear me the first time? Shall we get that sorted then? Shall we?'

'We'd rather not section him,' said the other one, who had a much more practical matter. 'We'd rather it was voluntary.'

'Is that all right, my love?' said Sweet Person. 'Bring you in for a little while? Get you back on your feet?'

Vic said nothing but I thought, 'Thank God.' I wasn't equipped to deal with this at all and I just wanted the experts to take over. It was a relief that they knew what to do, no matter how they were going about it. I got him out of the chair, helped him onto his feet, and guided him to the room as the Crisis Team members walked in front. Vic didn't seem as if he could harm anyone and no one had asked about the threats the voices had directed at me. He seemed so vulnerable. He felt floppy in my arms and had no life about him – this seemed like a different man to the vibrant, funny guy I had fallen for.

When we walked into the room, he said the first words since getting there.

'I need the toilet.'

'Of course you do,' said Sweet Person. 'Of course you do. We'll wait here for you. You just take your time – do what you have to do! No hurry at all, then we'll get things moving.'

It was the worst thing she could have done. She should have been watching him like a hawk, because as soon as he left the room he legged it. We were all waiting for him to come back and it took us about ten minutes to realise he'd gone. He must have just been waiting on an opportunity. Another member of the Crisis Team went to look for him, but there was no sign at all. They called the police, who also went looking for him, and I waited for an hour or so but nothing was happening. Eventually, they accepted he wouldn't come back or be found, so they suggested I go home and see if he turned up. I had told them all I knew about Vic's medical conditions while I waited. He had so many conditions to deal with, but had worked incessantly to bring them all under control and live as close to a normal life as he could. He was asthmatic and epileptic and autistic; but it was the last comment that made them sit up and take notice.

'Autistic? Being here would be a very bad idea for him, then,' the sensible team member said. 'It would be better if he could get help out of this setting. It's difficult to know what his main issues are – I would have expected him to present differently if autistic, but you never know.'

I went home and Vic was already there. I don't know how he had got in, as he didn't have a key, but he was curled up on the sofa looking very guilty and sheepish. He'd changed again. He was back to being childlike.

'I'm really sorry, Megan – am I in trouble?'

I went over and gave him a hug. 'Of course you're not in trouble. I'm just really worried about you, I'm not angry; this isn't your fault, but I want you to get better.'

He was like a naughty little boy who knew he had done something wrong. I genuinely couldn't have been cross.

'Are they going to take me away and lock me up?' he asked, quietly. 'Will they take me away from you? I don't want that. I want to stay here. You make me feel nice. I want to stay with you, please.'

I did what I could to reassure this poor, lost soul, then put him to bed. As I tucked the blankets around him, he said, 'Thank you, my love,' and I melted. How could life be so cruel? Vic had suffered so much already — surely he was due a break?

For a while the days weren't too bad but night times were tricky. That was when the voices came back. We got through it and I came to terms with the day-to-day realities of living with someone who has mental health issues. As if that wasn't enough to deal with, the email campaign against me continued. They were still saying the same things — slut, prostitute, porn star — but the fact that they came from so many different addresses horrified me as it certainly gave the impression that there were an awful lot of people trying to warn Vic against me. I knew that Christopher was behind it all, but how could I make Vic see that it was just one jealous ex-boyfriend?

'It doesn't matter, I know you're a good person,' he told me.

'But it's all lies,' I kept saying. 'I don't want you to say that it doesn't matter, because that sounds as if you think I am a whore, and I do porn – that's just not true. I want you to say you don't believe any of it and you trust me.'

'Of course I trust you,' he would say in his lucid days, but, to me, the emphasis was still on the wrong aspect of what was being said. I felt so lost, coping with so many things on my own, and being attacked by someone who I thought had loved me.

'Don't you worry about him,' said Vic. 'It'll get sorted – believe me, it'll get sorted.'

I didn't see how. My relationship with Christopher had ended badly and I had seen aspects of his personality at the end of our time together that I hated, and which, looking back, seemed like a precursor to what was now happening. When we started seeing each other, Christopher was very well-off; he had an incredibly successful business and more money than he knew what to do with. We had spent lots of time in expensive restaurants, ordering whatever we liked, and money was no object. He showered me with expensive gifts and enjoyed splashing out whenever the fancy took him. It didn't last. When the recession kicked in, his business suffered terribly and our lifestyle became one of waiting until things were reduced in the supermarket, or not knowing if the rent could be paid, rather than living like millionaires. I didn't care. I was with him because of how I felt, not because of the size of his wallet, but Christopher didn't see it that way. He became paranoid that I didn't love him any more, that he was too old, too ugly, and definitely too poor for me.

'I'm not bothered about that stuff at all – you must know that?' I said. 'It's what you feel that matters, not what you can buy.'

I might as well have been talking to the wall. He started following me when I went out, listening in to calls, accusing me of having affairs with people I had known for years. When we finally split up, he took back all of the gifts he had ever given me and even did petty things, like turning all the bottles of expensive toiletries I'd had as gifts upside down in the sink, so that I couldn't even use them.

In retrospect, the most chilling thing he did was to take back the laptop he'd given me. That, I now realised, had been the main focus of his behaviour – and that must have been when he loaded it with viruses and spyware. Christopher returned it to me after a couple of days, admitting he'd gone too far – saying he knew I needed it for work – but clearly he had achieved what he wanted during those few days it was in his possession. He must have been watching me since we'd split up and now he was intent on breaking up my new relationship.

I'd told Vic all of this soon after we met, and now he could see just how twisted Christopher was. I didn't know what I would have done without him and Martin to help me through all of this. It was testament to how well people thought of Vic that he always seemed to be able to call in favours, and I was just so grateful that he could still fight for me at a time when he was going through such troubles himself. I felt incredibly vulnerable but had to stay strong, as we never knew when the voices would come back and take Vic to a terrible place.

'I think Dina's death has tipped me over,' he confided quietly to me one night as we lay in bed. 'I think you're the only one who can save me, Megan, the only one.'

The truth was, we both needed help – we were both in trouble, and we would need to fight all of this together.

CHAPTER 5

IN TOO DEEP

November–December 2009

After talks with the Crisis Team at the Woodlands Clinic, it had been decided that Vic could stay with me, given that he was clearly stressed about being in their environment. The deal was that they would come and see him every day at my house rather than taking him as an in-patient. After he had run away when he had pretended to go to the loo, the likely course of action would have been to section him, so this seemed the best outcome. It was hoped that he would make more progress with me, but it was quite a responsibility. Our relationship was going so fast. We hadn't really known each other terribly long, but already we had revealed so much to each other and faced so many battles.

The home visits didn't last that long and were quite unsatisfactory. They seemed superficial and rarely occurred when Vic was at his worst, so he was discharged from the Crisis Team and assigned a psychiatrist for assessment. I got the impression that the service was massively under-staffed and that if there was any chance of offloading someone onto another area, they'd take it. For Vic, I thought it would have been better if he had been taken in, but he was adamant that he couldn't even consider this as his autism would make it so difficult to be around other people, and many of the medical staff agreed. He told that me he had to fight it every day so that he could continue with his DJing, and even being in regular contact with people, but a hospital situation would push him over the edge, perhaps permanently. He had so many things to battle, and I felt that if I could help him with this one thing by providing a listening ear and a safe environment, then it was the least I could do. I was quite scared and rather anxious to be taking on so much, but I cared deeply for Vic by now and wanted to help.

Vic was in a terrible way at home most of the time, going out walking every night and being instructed by the voices to do bad things to himself. I became too fretful to sleep myself, as I was worried about what he might do – the voices were so intense for him, what if his psyche just became too fragile and he gave in to them? It was immensely stressful, as I had Ruby to care for, a business to run, my ex still sending Vic these crazy emails, and now Vic's extreme mental disorder. He seemed to have gone completely mad and I felt like I had to stay up all night babysitting him. To be honest, he wasn't crazy all the time – he would seem to flip from being totally OK to utterly raving. He was generally much worse at night. He would sleep a lot during the day, which I tried to stop him from doing in a failed attempt to get normal sleeping patterns established. On more than one occasion I had to get the police involved to go and find him, as I would get a phone call from him at 2am or 3am in one of his states, not knowing where he was and telling me that the voices were telling him to jump off a building or hurt somebody or whatever it was that time. I would be unable to leave the house to go and find him myself, as I had Ruby there asleep. He hated it when I got the police involved – to him they were always 'pigs' – but to me they were a lifeline.

I tried to find some strategies to help him but they were few and far between; and, on the occasions I did happen across something that helped, there seemed to be no logic as to *why* it did. One thing that worked when he was having an episode was to start punching holes in paper with a hole-puncher. On one occasion when the police came round, an officer sat for hours with him as he went through sheets and sheets of paper putting holes in them. Vic also started talking about knives a lot of the time. The voices were telling him to hurt himself with knives, and a few times I found him with sharp knives from my kitchen in his hand or in his pocket. He said he was really afraid that he might hurt himself, so, one day, he asked me to hide the knives. My house had more than enough places to hide things so I didn't see it as a problem. Underneath one of the stairwells there was a cupboard where I kept towels and linen, and below the shelves there were no floorboards, with a recess going right back to the bottom of the stairs. I put all of the knives in a bag and threw the bag into the dark recess, out of sight and out of reach. I breathed a sigh of relief as I did it – that was one less thing to worry about.

The next morning, I went down to breakfast after getting Ruby started, and Vic was sat there, waiting for me, with the knives all laid out on the table in front of him.

'Jesus, Vic!' I exclaimed. 'How did you find them?'

'The voices told me. You can't keep anything from the voices. They heard me ask you to hide them, but they must have seen where you put them.'

I had no idea how this had happened and it freaked me out completely. I was coping with a five-year-old (who I had to protect from all of this), trying to run a business, the ongoing drama of Christopher sending abusive emails, and now Vic's increasing mental health problems.

Poor Vic, Valerie would message. *He's such a special person but he has so many burdens. It's good that you're there for him, Megan, he needs someone like you. He can achieve so much, and so many people recognise just how talented he is, but they don't see the demons he has to battle.*

Valerie – and, to a lesser extent, Leah and Clare – was a lifeline to me. She was online at all hours of the day and night, especially night due to her crazy work patterns.

Hectic here! she would say from Spain or Portugal or somewhere in Eastern Europe. *How are things with you?*

It was very different at home – no music, no parties, no DJing lifestyle, just me wondering when Vic would go mad again, and trying to protect a little girl in the middle of it all. So often I would finally get Vic to calm down at about 3am, finally convince him that he was safe, and I would go to bed and FB chat with Valerie, knowing that Vic was conked out in another room. I relied on her a great deal and wished that we could meet in person; but as she was rarely even in the country, I knew it wasn't likely at the moment.

Vic's troubles had brought a change in our relationship in many ways. He could still be kind and gentle, I still saw flashes of the man I had fallen for so quickly, but what there was between us had altered dramatically as soon as he had his first episode of madness. He no longer wanted to share a room with me as he was so disturbed at night, so he moved into one of the spare rooms. Really, I had gone from being his girlfriend to being his carer. I had no idea how I was going to get myself out of this situation, but I knew it was no way for me to live long term. I was also very much aware, just as I'd been with Lucas and Christopher, that Ruby needed a good role model. It wouldn't be a fantastic blueprint for her to see me do nothing with my life, just be weighed down with someone else's battles.

I wouldn't say I was planning to leave Vic, but I didn't see it as a permanent relationship. I hoped that he would get the medical support he needed for his mental health when he felt a little stronger – if I could help him to get that strength we'd both be in a better place. So, I told myself, perhaps when he knew that he could fight this effectively he would be more open to accepting medication and maybe even become an in-patient at the Woodlands Clinic until he was back on his feet. He hated it when I suggested anything like that, and I knew he must be mentioning it to the girls at the collective as they would often raise the issue, albeit sometimes in a less obvious way.

It's great that u are standing by Vic, hun, typed Clare. *So many ppl just av no sense of loyalty. He deserves better than that. U are a star. I no that u will get such a gr8 life with him if u stand by and keep standing by him cos he is a gr8 guy xx*

It was as if she had read my mind and knew we were having problems. I sometimes felt so guilty for even thinking of a future without him, but I wasn't planning to bale out straight away, just in the future, once he was back on his feet. The truth was, I wanted more from a relationship. I was still young, I still wanted love and passion. I didn't want to just be someone's carer. I wanted a life.

I also wanted the online harassment to stop. Christopher had ramped things up a notch and had contacted Vic's niece, Willow. She was now receiving all of the emails saying that I was a slut and a prostitute – and she had gleefully passed them all on to Vic's sister, Kat. They were revelling in the fact that he had hooked up with someone outside their community who had turned out to be so horrible, lacking in any morals whatsoever, and completely shaming to him. Christopher must have hacked into all of Vic's personal stuff to be able to contact Willow in the first place. She was a stunningly beautiful young woman who was doing really well with a modelling career – Vic had shown me pictures of shoots she had done, and told me she was destined for amazing things. However, there was no way Christopher would have been able to contact her through any public option (people like her don't exactly broadcast their personal email addresses!) and, anyway, she used a different name for work for fear that people would connect her to her Romany family and she'd face bigotry. No, Christopher knew exactly who she was and told her all of the lies (through the many email addresses to make it look as if plenty of people were sending out warnings) that Vic had been subjected to as well.

I wasn't surprised at all when Vic told me that Willow had passed everything on to her mother, the terrifying Kat, who had let her own younger daughter die, and who now had me in her sights. Even though Vic had left his family roots behind, they were always trying to drag him back in. If he mixed with anyone they didn't approve of – which was pretty much anyone without a Romany background – he would soon hear about it. As well as the deluge of emails from Christopher, Vic now had to cope with Kat telling him he was a disgrace for hooking up with a slag like me, and 'the family' wanted it sorted out sooner rather than later.

As far as they were all concerned, I was indeed a prostitute and Vic was blinded by love. They never left him alone, telling him I was a terrible person and he needed to get away from me. He was so different to the rest of them, but I wondered how much more he could take. Sometimes I thought it would be the lies that would split us up, and that, if so, I would just have to accept it. Obviously, I would rather people didn't believe horrendous lies about me, but I couldn't exactly fight back against anonymous evil. Vic seemed stronger when he was fighting my corner. When he was helping me, in times of real crisis, he managed to shake off the voices and respond in a really great way. It straightened his head out and he would seem more like the man I had originally met; but, every so often, something would come through to remind me how things really were.

'Nice Lady says you're having a baby,' Vic told me one day. We were sitting on the sofa. He was hearing voices but not in the scary way – in the way where he seemed more like a vulnerable child. He started stroking my belly. 'Nice Lady says I have to look after you.'

'That's just silly,' I replied, reminding him that we didn't really have sex any more. 'I'm not having a baby, it's just nonsense talk.'

'No, Nice Lady says it's true. Is it mine?' he asked.

'I'm not pregnant! But I can assure you that if the world was turned upside down and I was, you would be the father.' The very fact that he was asking made me wonder whether he did have a niggling doubt about all of Christopher's emails. Of course I wasn't pregnant, but if it had been an option, would Vic have questioned the paternity?

'Nice Lady says you have a baby in there. She wouldn't lie.'

'I don't think Nice Lady is right about this,' I told him gently. 'I'm definitely not having a baby.'

I tried to push it out of my mind.

I definitely wasn't pregnant, and in any case there was no woman in Vic's head who had a special way of looking into me and passing on the information. That was the truth of it all. I. Was. Not. Pregnant.

Except … I was.

Just when I thought things couldn't get any worse, towards the end of November, Vic's prophecy came true.

We'd had unprotected sex on day eight of my cycle – I remembered that because it was a rare occurrence by then. Vic had some problems with sex, and it was very unusual for it to reach a stage where I could even potentially have got pregnant anyway, so I hadn't worried about it in the slightest. I wasn't on edge for the rest of the month, I didn't think I needed the morning-after pill – it hadn't seemed an issue. Then my period was late.

Nice Lady's words ran through my mind as I checked my diary. Late. Late. Late. I was never late. Or, more accurately, I'd only ever been late once before and she was now five years old!

I bought a twin pack of pregnancy tests from the supermarket that day and plucked up the courage to do one as soon as I got back. Perched on the edge of the bath, I watched the second hand go round on the clock and cursed myself for being so silly. It couldn't possibly be positive – I ran through all the reasons … very little sex, hardly ever sex that ended in a way that I could get pregnant, last time on day eight.

I took a deep breath and looked.

Negative.

Of course it was negative, I scolded myself, of course it was. I gave myself the same ticking off a few days later when my period still hadn't arrived. 'Stress can do that,' I whispered to my reflection in the bathroom mirror as I waited for the minutes to tick by again. 'I'm sure that the more you worry about it, the more likely it is to stay away.'

I looked at the line. Just the one line. I was right again.

Negative.

But still my period didn't come. I'd never missed one in my life before, so what was going on? I bought another test, just to prove to myself that I was definitely right, and then I thought I'd go to my GP, just to see why my periods had suddenly stopped. I didn't really pay attention to that one, keeping myself busy as the minutes passed by. I glanced down at the test on my way to tidying up the bathroom towels. This one was the type that told you in words, as I wanted to see it for sure, wanted to know that I was right.

Positive.

Two to three weeks pregnant.

I fell down onto the floor.

How could that be? How could I get two negatives, then this? More than anything, I was freaked out that Nice Lady had known this before me. How could an imaginary voice in Vic's head know I was pregnant? I hadn't even done a test when he made that comment.

Vic was hardly euphoric when I told him.

'I'm really worried about this, Megan Henley,' he told me, slipping back into his habit of affectionately calling me by my full name. I used to find that so endearing, but now it tended to indicate that Vic was feeling threatened or under pressure. I was worried too. I had no desire for another child whatsoever, but what with Vic's mental state and the fact that he had lost Zack and then Dina, I felt it would be too heartless to not go ahead with the pregnancy. I obviously had grave doubts about the future of my relationship with him, but I could see from the way he was with Ruby and the way he spoke about Zack and Dina that he adored kids, and I was pretty certain that, if nothing else, he would be so glad to be a parent again that even if it didn't work out between us he would be a good dad. Whenever Ruby was around he was always completely normal and she really liked him; it was generally only after she was asleep that he would have his episodes, and occasionally during the day while she was at school. So I thought that a baby, although totally unplanned, would be a way for him to get out of this terrible place he was in mentally, and give him a reason to live and to get better.

Everyone else seemed to agree.

'So happy for u, hun!' messaged Clare. *'Just what Vic needs, sumthing 2 focus on and make him happy. This is just wot he needs, make sure he feels like a special daddy xx'*

Valerie was even more certain. *'Finally, something to give our boy a bit of light in his life, a bit of hope for the future. You have no idea how this could change everything for him, Megan, no idea at all. I'm thrilled and know that Vic will be an amazing dad – he's so good around kids. I'm actually quite jealous, wish it was me!'*

'A baby is a very good idea,' said Leah bluntly. *'Well done. It will be good for him.'*

It was nice that they were all so supportive, but I also felt just a little bit steamrollered. Even if I had considered ending the pregnancy, how would I have coped with all of this outpouring of concern for Vic? Even Valerie saying that she wished it was her made me realise that, actually, I was really lucky. The thing was, the collective was happy – but they weren't the only ones in the picture. When Vic's family found out, the shit hit the fan.

You are fucking kidding, Unca? Willow messaged. *Having a kid with that two-bit whore? A fucking gorja? She's trying to trap you, Unca – ditch her, ditch that slag, she's probably lying anyway.*

They always referred to me as a 'gorja', a really derogatory name for a non-gypsy. The idea that Vic was having a child with someone who wasn't from the same background as them was completely unacceptable. I think they always hoped that he would see sense, in their eyes, and come back into the fold. Having a baby with a gorja made that even less likely, but, to his credit, Vic was supportive even though anxious.

'I can't face losing another child,' he told me. 'That terrifies me, Megan. I can't face the same as Zack all over again.'

'That won't happen,' I said, reassuringly. 'You see that I'm a good mother, you see how loved and safe and happy Ruby is – it'll be the same with our baby. I won't neglect it, I'll never put it in danger. You needn't worry on that score.'

Valerie was there when I needed someone to talk to about these things. *You'll be fine*, she messaged. *You've got him through everything so far and you'll be stronger together than his family. This is the start of something wonderful.*

If that was going to be the case, I wished it would begin soon. We were struggling to get by, as Vic's mental health problems meant that he couldn't work too much. He and the other members of StreetBeats generated a huge amount of money, and royalties, but they took only their expenses from the group, sending the rest to support projects in Zimbabwe. It was an honourable thing to do, but we were pretty badly off as a result.

'I need it to be this way,' Vic explained. 'I need it all to happen in Zack's memory and to know that his life wasn't wasted. If I can help other kids, kids with nothing, then I'll feel that I've achieved something in Zack's name.'

I could hardly whinge about that; it was such a noble thing to do. With the help of the local Citizens Advice Bureau, Vic went about claiming disability benefits for his mental health problems in an effort to contribute a bit more to the family pot. He was certainly in a terrible state when we went for the assessments. So often, when he could hear voices and things were at their worst, he would fixate on something and had no filter. When we left for the meeting that morning, he had actually seemed quite well, but, as soon as we went into the room where assessors were to talk to him, things changed. He curled up in a chair that he dragged to the furthest corner and refused to make eye contact. He was shaking like a terrified animal, and not answering any of their questions. I did what I could, but his only contribution was, halfway through, to shout, 'I need a poo!'

It would no doubt sound comical to anyone who didn't know the context but it was actually quite scary.

He was so loud, and so intent on just shouting this, over and over again, that I knew he was really struggling. It wasn't funny at all. Thankfully, the assessors could see that things were bad and he got the highest rates of benefit after that. Previously, we had been living off my earnings, which weren't that great, and royalties from an old band that Vic had been in, which was £200 paid into his account every fortnight, but now his benefits were increased and the financial side of things was a lot easier.

Even if he had been in perfect mental health, he would have been struggling with the pressure coming from his family. There was rarely a day when they didn't contact him to remind him where he came from, to ask for his help with dealing with someone, to try and lure him back into their shady business. I couldn't repeat any of that to the health professionals, but it must have all affected Vic. Luckily, Valerie was party to it all and I could always trust her and rely on her to be a sounding post. She was close to several members of Vic's family and could see the full picture. While Vic was always very secretive about that side of things, Valerie was usually happy to fill me in on the details of what was really going on.

You wouldn't believe the hassle he gets from them, she said. *He's such a good man, but I've told him he should share with you so you know just how much pressure he's under. He says no — you just need to concentrate on that baby, and he'll deal with everything else. It must be so reassuring to know someone has your back like that, Megan — take care and keep well.*

It was reassuring to some extent, because Vic did cope well when he was in a corner, but I just wished we could be left alone in peace — without all the pressure from his family, from the voices in his head, and from Christopher.

CHAPTER 6

DANGER

December 2009–July 2010

Christopher was furious about how things had panned out, and wasn't going to let anything lie. The emails and messages continued, and I couldn't settle. There was always a knot of worry in my stomach and I wasted far too much time wishing I'd never set eyes on him.

One night, I fell asleep on the sofa, exhausted by stress more than anything, much more than by the pregnancy. I don't think I'd been asleep more than five minutes when I felt Vic shaking my arm.

'Wake up, Megan,' he whispered. 'Stay quiet.'

My eyes were open in a second. They felt gritty and heavy, but the tone of Vic's voice made me instantly realise that I couldn't wallow in sleepiness.

'What's wrong?' I hissed.

'Someone's outside. Get upstairs. Turn all the lights off. And hide. Get Ruby and hide. Don't phone the police.'

'Are you sure? Are you sure someone's outside?' I asked.

'Of course I'm sure. I've been sitting here watching over you while you slept and I heard someone. Someone's in the garden. They've been pacing around, checking the doors, so you just get upstairs, get Ruby and hide. I'll deal with this.'

Ruby's room was on the top floor so I went up there, quickly but quietly. If Vic had heard someone outside, I had no reason to linger downstairs with something bad maybe about to happen. I sat outside Ruby's room in case anyone did get past him and came into the house; I'd protect Ruby to my last breath if I had to.

Vic had gone outside, to chase whoever was out there, but I could tell by the wind that he had left the back door open. I heard him shouting and was now terrified – I expected to hear someone come back in the house at any second; I just wouldn't know who it would be. Sitting on the stairs, in the dark, fully prepared to hurt anyone who came near my child, pregnant and terrified – I wondered how my life had turned into a horror story. I wanted to call the police, I desperately wanted to call them, but he'd told me not to and I had to trust him. I sat there in the pitch black terrified for Ruby, for me, my unborn baby and for Vic, who had disappeared into the garden to find out who was there. I was sure it was my ex, or someone sent by my ex. I sat there absolutely petrified for what felt like an age, knowing that the back door was open, so if there was an altercation and Vic came off worse, then whoever was in the garden could come into the house and I would have no way of protecting myself or Ruby.

My heart was pounding by the time I heard the door bang and Vic's voice shout, 'Megan! It's fine! All sorted!'

I belted down the stairs and threw myself into his arms. He was out of breath but seemed to be pumped up on adrenalin rather than fear.

'What happened? My God, Vic, what happened out there?' I asked.

He was breathing heavily as he told me. 'When I got out to the garden, whoever it was ran down to the bottom. They got out of the gate and I chased him up the hill into the village. I managed to catch him there and … well, let's just say he'll be sorry he messed with me.'

'You hit him?'

Vic nodded. 'Of course I did. He was on my turf, Megan. Decking him was a lot less than I wanted to do.'

'Where is he? Where did he go?' I asked, then, 'Vic – who was it?'

'There was a car waiting for him – it must have all been set up, it wasn't just someone chancing their luck as they went past. It was no bog-standard burglar look-ing for an open door, Megan.'

'This has gone too far,' I said, wiping some blood off his cheek. I picked up the phone and started calling 999.

Vic grabbed it out of my hand. 'No, Megan – you're right that it's gone too far, but this needs to be dealt with by my family, not some poxy copper who sticks to the rules and doesn't know what he's really facing.'

I was still, at heart, a nice middle-class girl – for me, when things went wrong, or bad guys were involved, you called the police. 'But Vic,' I said, 'we need to get the police involved so this can be stopped.'

'It will get stopped, Megan, it will.'

'Please, Vic, please let me call them,' I begged.

He sighed. 'I'm telling you, it'll do no good but …' he waved his arm at the phone, 'go ahead – be my guest.'

They came round really quickly, checked the premises to see if there was someone hanging around – but we knew there wasn't. Vic had said that he had seen a car that matched Christopher's, but there was no sign of that either.

'Can you tell me what happened, sir?' asked one of the officers.

'I chased a man wearing a balaclava out of the garden and across the road, caught up with the man and had a few words with him, then the man got up and ran down the hill to a car that was waiting with its engine running and then sped off,' he told them, leaving out the fact that he'd punched him as hard as he could. The police could find nothing. It wasn't surprising that there was no evidence, and it really just backed up what Vic had said – the police could do nothing.

'I hate to say it, but I told you so,' he said when they left. 'I'll never let anyone harm you. You mean the world to me, but you need to let me deal with it on my terms in the ways I know best.'

'Vic, you already have so much to deal with – it's just unfair that you have to cope with my psycho ex as well. Do you think he's still out there watching us?'

'No – I sent him on his way. But who knows what he might try next?'

We didn't have to wait long to find out.

The next night the same thing happened. I had been putting Ruby to bed and dozed off – probably before her. I was so dopey with pregnancy hormones that I would drop off anywhere. I woke with a start when I heard a door banging downstairs.

'Vic!' I shouted.

There was no reply.

I crept downstairs and, again, the kitchen door was wide open. Not long after I got there Vic came back in, sweating and out of breath.

'Same guy, I'm sure of it,' he said. 'Balaclava, same build as last night. He took the same route as well, but he was quicker tonight – he got away without a scratch on him, the lucky bastard.'

'I'm calling the police,' I said, grabbing my mobile. 'It's one thing to send nasty emails, it's another to do this.'

Vic snatched the phone away from me. 'Fuck the police. This has gone beyond the police now. This is going to be dealt with by my family. I'll tell you again; it's gone beyond the police, Megan – you must see that. Your ex isn't going to listen to them; they'd probably never even catch him. This needs to be dealt with by my family. Understand?' I was a bag of nerves. I didn't have the strength to argue about it – what if this went on and on throughout my whole pregnancy? What if it was still happening when the baby got here? How far would Christopher go?

Vic put his coat on and left for the payphone. He always went into the village to call from there if he was dealing with anything dodgy or that he wanted to keep from me. I sat outside Ruby's room, as was becoming my habit, and waited until he got back before venturing downstairs again.

All he said was, 'It's being dealt with.'

I felt as if it was all divided into goodies and baddies; it was ridiculous. On the good guy side, as well as Vic and the collective, there was also Uncle Alan. Brother of Vic's dad, Alan couldn't have been more different. He completely supported Vic's attempts to break away and helped him whenever he could. He had a yard in Liverpool and I also suspected that he gave Vic money when he was really desperate. I could never make my mind up about Vic's mum, Isabella. She turned a blind eye to everything his father did and I had a sense that Vic still really loved her. When he was a child, although she didn't remove him from the situation, she would do all she could to make it better. Vic portrayed it as a very traditional gypsy set-up. What the man said went as law – her job was to clean and cook and serve. That was what she had been born into, so she didn't see anything wrong with that.

They had been together since his mum was thirteen and his dad was fifteen. Basically, Jay came from a family of gypsies who were part of a travelling fair. They went all around Europe with it and were once in the Basque region of Spain. Vic's mum, Isabella, was a local gypsy girl, and when she came to the fair his dad took a shine to her and a deal was done between the two families that she would go with them when they left. Vic was born not too long after that, which was shocking. After they got together, Vic's dad left the fair and they all lived on a travellers' site near London. She was only fourteen when he was born. Vic was born in a Westmoreland Star gypsy caravan, a beautiful place with glass and chrome, which cost a fortune and only the highest Roma could afford.

I didn't really know too much about the good side of his family but I was aware that there were far too many of them on the bad guy list. That night, when he came back from the phone box, I knew that those on that list were involved.

Life carried on in a similar way, threats coming from left, right and centre, Vic having severe problems with the voices in his head, me in the last few weeks of pregnancy. It was a right struggle handling all this, it was like living in a gangster film, and it didn't help that Vic had cut me off from all my friends. He told me that it was too dangerous to have people round who didn't understand what was going on, and he also didn't want me shouting my mouth off to all and sundry. I needed a break from him sometimes. I had several friends living in the town, but if I made plans to meet any of them Vic would suddenly take a turn for the worse, mentally, just before I was about to go, and I would be unable to leave him. It got to the point where I had no life at all, aside from him and Ruby.

The next big drama came in February. I had spent most of my pregnancy in fear and often only felt safe when I was in bed, reading. It was quite late at night when he came into my room – we were still in separate beds, in separate parts of the house, and I had accepted that was just how it had to be. I needed him for protection, and I had to make allowances for how he was. That night I could tell just from looking at him that he was suffering badly with his voices.

'Are you OK, love?' I asked.

'I've been to church today, Megan Henley,' he said, quietly.

'Well, that's nice,' I replied. 'Was it quiet?'

'I lit three candles,' he told me, solemnly. 'One for Zack, one for Dina, one for Logan.'

I didn't understand why he would light one for Logan, who was Kat's second youngest child who was fifteen.

'Is Logan poorly?' I queried.

'No. Not yet.'

'Why did you light a candle for him, then?'

'I saw it, Megan Henley. He fell. I saw it.'

'What? Today? You saw Logan fall today?' I asked. I found it pretty unlikely that he had spent any time with Kat or one of her kids.

'He fell, Megan Henley,' he went on. 'There was a big wall with a big drop on the other side and he fell. Logan fell. He'll die, so I had to light a candle for him.'

It all seemed a bit far-fetched to me and I assumed he was just talking rubbish, but the next day I was on Facebook when Valerie popped up online.

Megan, I can't get Vic online but I need to get a message to him. Can you tell him that there's been an accident? His nephew, Logan, has been really badly hurt. He's in hospital in Manchester. Ask Vic if he wants to visit – I'm sure Kat would appreciate it.

I was shocked and asked what had happened.

Logan fell off a high wall last night – God knows what he was doing. He's broken his legs and pelvis, and has awful head injuries. He's in a coma, Megan – Vic needs to know. Family comes first, no matter what.

This wasn't possible! How could Vic have seen this before it happened? How could the voices in his head tell him all about it? He was wrong in that Logan hadn't died, but everything else … I had no idea how this could be. It was as if he could never escape from his family. The investigation into Dina's death was ongoing, and, on a few occasions, Vic had to travel to Manchester to be interviewed by the police, and give evidence at court hearings. It turned out that, shockingly, she had been found to have over two grams of cocaine in her system when she died. The poor driver who hit her gave evidence saying that she appeared from nowhere and ran straight in front of the car. There was no time to brake, and just before the car hit her Dina looked the driver in the eye and made the sign of the cross. It transpired, although this was something Vic had found out 'behind the scenes' rather than through court, that Dina's own mother, Kat, was responsible for her death. Although she hadn't been present at the time, from what I could gather Kat had arranged for Dina to be force-fed the drugs as some sort of punishment for bad behaviour. Although it appeared that Dina had run in front of the car herself, Vic hinted that she had been forced into doing this. Kat had skipped the country using a fake passport, and now that the investigation had come to such a horrifying conclusion she was wanted by the police.

And now there was Logan too. He was in hospital for a month in a coma. Tests showed that he too had high amounts of Class A drugs in his system when he had the fall. Through the grapevine Vic discovered that his sister Kat was behind this 'accident' too. It turned out that Logan had stolen a few thousand pounds from her, so this was her payback. From what I understood Logan had been injected with all these drugs, forced up onto the wall, then either pushed or made to jump.

As the weeks went on, I knew that Vic hadn't been to see Logan. It was heartbreaking for him, but he had to make a choice.

'My future's with you and this little one,' he said, gently stroking my growing bump. 'I can't go back, I can't be dragged into it all.'

'You are already,' I reminded him, pointing out that he had been dragged back due to all the hassle with Christopher. 'They have you already.'

'That's different,' he claimed. 'That's to protect you and Ruby and the baby. I'll do anything for you three, but, as much as I loved Logan, Kat has made her bed there.'

The next day, Logan had a massive heart attack and died. Vic had never seen him again. I started to panic about my unborn baby, fearing for the future for any child born into this horrifically dysfunctional family. All of Vic's information was now coming through Valerie and Willow. Although he kept telling me that no one would ever hurt our baby, I didn't feel safe, I didn't feel I was being protected. From what Vic told me, Willow in particular had it in for me – when she wasn't telling her mum that I was a whore, she was telling her grandmother. I couldn't understand why they even had anything to do with their parents, given what had been done to Willow as a teenager. I felt totally unnerved, several children in this family having suffered horrible deaths. I was also very worried about ever meeting any of his family members – Willow and Vic's mum certainly seemed to have it in for me, which was bad enough, but Vic's dad and Kat were the ones I really didn't want to meet by the sound of things, although I hadn't had any direct threats from them. The stories about his dad were awful – he connected with criminals the world over, from Triads to Yardies. I hoped to be able to keep out of his line of fire for ever.

All the stalking by Christopher came to a head the next month. I had been having counselling every week – it was meant to be hypnobirthing sessions, as I was anxious about giving birth, but that worry had paled into insignificance compared to all the other stresses. For an hour every week I would just let go of it all and be in floods of tears about all these people who were out to get me, and the stress of having to deal with Vic's mental health problems. Vic had been having Christopher followed for some time and knew quite a lot about what he got up to, and had also hacked Christopher's computers to see what he was looking at. Vic told me that Christopher had gone to a swinger's club in Birmingham and Vic had some of his 'associates' follow him there. They filmed him having sex with people, then sent the DVD of the footage to Christopher's ex-wife, who was the mother of his three children. Vic believed that this would send a clear message to Christopher that we were not to be messed with and that it should result in him leaving us alone. If his ex-wife chose to, she could use the DVD to claim that he was an unsuitable father and possibly even stop him getting access.

When it didn't actually do anything to stop him at all, Vic got angrier and angrier. I started to communicate again with Vic's friend Martin, the forensic computer expert. He initially contacted me to apologise for the lack of contact and to explain what was happening re my own laptop.

Hello Megan – I was asked by Vic a little while ago to drop you a line re your computer. Sorry it has taken so long to respond but my workload of late has been, well let's say strenuous! He mentioned you have some doubts etc re your stalker still possibly hacking into your account. Although I can't really explain it in layman's terms as it is very compli- cated, I will say there is no chance that this person can hijack any of your passwords etc; your computer is very safe. You may notice from time to time that, when you check your history, there may be a few extra items within the page – please do not worry, that is either myself doing some maintenance or what is known as a mirror draft; again, it is hard to explain but I can assure you everything is how it should be and, of course, if anything goes wrong please don't hesitate to email me. I would like to take this opportunity to congratulate yourself and Vic on your baby news. Fantastic stuff, hope all goes well when the little one gets here! Please say hi to Vic from me. All the best, Martin

I was reassured by his words, and glad to know that Vic had someone else looking out for me even when I didn't know it.

Hi Martin, I replied, *thanks very much for all your efforts so far, I really appreciate it. And thanks re the baby, we are both very happy about it and Vic is being very sweet and looking after me! Thought I'd better drop you a line as my ex is definitely in my computer again. Firstly I noticed a few days ago that a message that I was sent on Facebook was deleted before I read it, I only knew I had received it as a copy was sent to my Hotmail account and I saw it there.*

The same person who sent me that message had been deleted off my friends list, and I didn't delete him and he didn't delete me. My ex has been emailing Vic's niece stirring all sorts of shit and trying to make out that I have been cheating on Vic. Luckily Vic knows this isn't true but unfortunately now both Vic's mum and his niece won't speak to him unless he finishes with me because apparently I am a porn star and a prostitute among other things (news to me!), so it's not good. Christopher is definitely still snooping around. Hope that makes sense, all a bit confusing! I know he has several computers and uses a Vodaphone dongle to use the internet most of the time, whether he has a broadband connection on his land-line, I am not sure. Also Valerie tells me that Willow told her that he is bugging my mobile phone. I had a quick look on the internet and there seems to be software you can download to do this with, do you know anything about this kind of thing and what I can do about it? Thanks again, Megan

The next message from Martin was entitled 'Your Hacker':

Hi Megan – sorry it has took me an age to reply to your last email but family commitments etc have got in the way of everything over the last few weeks. I see Vic has installed Windows 7 on your system and what a fantastic job he has done on it (I taught him well lol). There is no way anybody is going to get into your new system the way it has been set up. I only got in because Vic give me the relevant codes etc.

What I would suggest though is that, although it is a right pain, delete your history at the end of each day, this stops any activity by hackers tenfold, and also if you have any photos music etc that have been installed from your old system onto your new one, it might be an idea to either put them onto an external hard drive, change the serial numbers on them or even delete them, these type of files and folders are a very easy way for hackers to store information about you. As regarding your hacker I have seen no activity within the last 3 weeks that he is doing anything to your computer at all so I am a little mystified on that one. I will have a closer look on Monday and let you know if I find anything. You need to be aware that hackers do pass information on and because there were such big holes in your last system unfortunately it has been open to abuse for any of these stupidly inclined people. As I mentioned earlier your new system is top drawer stuff. There is not even an encryption code for people to copy so I would feel a lot easier about using your computer. Cheers, Martin

The thought that Christopher was passing on all of my personal details to other nutters was horrible. I cursed myself again for not being a better judge of character. At least, this time, with Vic, I had someone who would fight my corner. Even when we were arguing between ourselves, I told myself it was just natural as we had a new baby on the way – the fact was, even when we niggled, he had my back. To begin with, he'd known nothing about computers, that was why he had got Martin involved in the first place, and now he had taught himself so much just in order to help me. Even Martin was impressed!

I didn't have a chance to relax for long, though, as another message popped through a couple of days later:

Hi Megan – just to let you know there was some strange activity on your Facebook last night. Someone it would seem was trying to change your password. Don't worry though they didn't get past the first mirror and I have checked it this morning and it is all running fine. If you have any problems please let me know. Thanks – Martin.

'Does this guy not know who I fucking am?' Vic asked. 'Why is he not getting the message? It's time for this to stop.' With this, he headed out to the public phone box again – in fact, for the next few days it felt like he was there more than he was at home.

Nothing was ever specifically said to me, as Vic didn't believe I could keep my mouth shut, but all of the clues led me to believe that a big, covert gypsy operation was being planned and that Christopher was going to be bumped off. I couldn't believe it had got that far, but it also seemed so far that there was no turning back, if that made sense. I was pregnant and vulnerable – and I kept my head down.

'He won't be bothering you any more,' Vic told me one day, holding me tightly in his arms, and being more affectionate that I could remember in a long while. I didn't dare ask how he could be so certain about that, I just felt a massive sense of relief that the months of being stalked by Christopher were over. Sure enough, Vic was right. An almost pleasant few months followed, from the spring onwards, where it seemed we were getting minimal bother from Vic's family. I suffered really bad pelvic pain during my pregnancy, and Vic was a real help. I was pretty much unable to walk, but he would happily take Ruby to school and back so that I could get some rest. We were very definitely not in a conventional relationship, he had his room and I had mine, but the impending baby seemed to have given Vic a focus and a reason to not be mad, and his mental health problems were pretty much all better. I had a horrible feeling, though, that all this was the calm before the storm where his family were concerned.

The improvements in Vic's mental health meant that he started up a business doing computer repairs. He'd learned so much from Martin when the online harassment had started from Christopher that he said it would be a waste not to do something with it. He put adverts and cards around the town and soon the work started coming in. Vic seemed able to fix computers that had been declared dead by other repair places, and had many happy customers. He told me that he would enter the BIOS settings of the computer and talk to it using code, which would entice it back to life – he explained that he had been able to learn it really quickly because of his autism. It was all another language to me, but it also seemed like a fantastic step on the way to a normal life.

There was one thing I found confusing about it all, though – Vic had told me that he had a condition called synaesthesia. This is a neurological condition which has a lot of different forms. In one type of synaesthesia, signs, letters and numbers take on the form of colours to the sufferer, and this is what Vic had. With this, for example, the numbers zero and one could be white and black, and the letter 'A' could be red. Vic had told me that it meant he could only read text if it was in certain colours, and the colour he found easiest was green writing on a red background. He told me that his own laptop had been installed with a programme which meant that he could read text on it and that he had been helped by a special support group for people who had synaesthesia. However, he seemed to have absolutely no problem in using other people's computers for hours on end while he was fixing them; I couldn't work it out, but assumed it was just part of the mental health issues he battled daily, and that I was privileged to not have to deal with such things in my own life.

I patted my belly as I thought about all of Vic's troubles, and tried to ignore the awful things he had done just to keep us safe.

'Soon,' I told the little one growing inside me, 'soon you'll be here, and I'll have the strength to concentrate on just making a wonderful life for you. Wonderful, but normal. Very, very normal.'

It was all I wished for. A healthy baby, a safe family life, and blissful normality. I might as well have been asking for the moon on a stick.

CHAPTER 7

SILENCE

July 2010 – January 2011

We were also planning to move house. The place we'd found in Horsham was much nicer than the cottage, which held so many bad memories for me, and I hoped it would be a fresh start. There were four bedrooms, which meant we could keep our current arrangement of separate rooms, which seemed important to Vic. The only problem was that the move ended up being very close to my due date. Luckily, in some ways, my little girl decided to arrive early.

As I was packing up the old house, the contractions started. I'd been here before, so I decided to just keep going with boxing things up and go to hospital as late as possible. I had a doula ready on speed dial to meet me there, and was hoping for as little intervention as possible. I was so worried that Vic might have an episode when I went into labour, which was why I had engaged a doula in the first place; I needed someone I could rely on. Life had been so crazy, but I desperately wanted this little one to come out into peace and calm.

Ruby was with her dad. I held on for as long as I could, and then, with the contractions mounting, Vic drove me to hospital. He was chatty on the way there, playing me music that he'd been working on and trying to help with my breathing. However, as soon as we were shown into the labour room, he changed. We were met by Magda, the doula, and he disappeared almost immediately.

'Where are you going?' I shouted as he headed out of the door.

'Need to move the car!' he replied. 'Don't want a ticket.'

This went on all through the labour. He seemed obsessed with moving the car to avoid a traffic warden seeing it, and ignored my perfectly sensible advice to 'JUST PAY FOR A BLOODY SPACE!!' A pregnant woman in the last throes of labour is perhaps not the most reasonable person in the world, but I did feel that he was being absolutely ridiculous. Thankfully, I had Magda with me and she was more help than Vic could ever have been. The contractions were coming quickly, and agonisingly, and the last thing I could be bothered with was Vic's odd ways. I clung on to Magda and promised myself that I would NEVER be doing this again. Finally, it was over – one last push, one last scream and there she was.

My little girl.

My Lily.

She was stunning. All dark hair and big lungs. Vic was there for it, for the most important part, and he was in tears when she arrived. I knew that he must be thinking of Zack – and probably Dina and Logan too. He had previously said to me that he wouldn't have a minute's peace until the baby got past the age of Zack, but I kept reassuring him that I was very different to Zack's mother and no one would put my children in danger, least of all me.

We spent that night in hospital, just the three of us, closed off from the world. I was able to tell myself that once we got home – to our new house – we could press a reset button and be all the things I desperately wanted us to be. I sang to Lily, I bathed her, I cuddled her and kissed her but, from the start, she was a handful. She was extremely fractious and unsettled as a baby, and, as I was breastfeeding, there wasn't much Vic could do during the nights. She would wake up at least once an hour (and this went on until she was eight months old). Vic was a doting dad; he clearly adored her and loved taking her for walks in the pram. I knew that he must be thinking about Zack and it must have been hard for him. Lily was an absolutely gorgeous child and I think that Vic – like all parents! – loved it when people commented on how beautiful she was.

Ruby turned out to be a brilliant big sister and I would often look at my two girls and think I was absolutely blessed. 'You are my little wonders,' I told them. 'Nothing, nothing will ever harm you.' I meant it – no matter what life threw at us, I would always be there for them.

I hoped that some time after Lily's birth the physical side of my relationship with Vic would get back on track. He had chosen to sleep in a separate room ever since he first became acutely unwell with his mental health problems and, while I tried to understand this, I wondered why it was still the case. His experiences with the voices seemed few and far between, but he continued to have no interest in any sort of physical contact with me. I attributed it to the fact that I had put on weight while I was pregnant, but I was extremely hurt that he would not even give me a cuddle if I asked him to. Any time that I tried to broach this subject or initiate any intimacy, the result wasn't good.

'Why are you always on about sex?' he'd ask, even although that was far from the truth. 'My head is in a complete fucking mess with thinking about Zack and Dina and Logan and all you can think about is whether you can get me in your knickers. Get a fucking grip, will you?' He made me feel really bad for even bringing it up and didn't seem to grasp that sex was a normal part of a healthy adult relationship. 'You're not helping anything, Megan,' he would say. 'You have no idea how many things I'm dealing with right now. I protect you from so much, and all you can think of is how to stress me out asking for sex. It's fucking ridiculous, it really is.'

'So, tell me, Vic, talk to me,' I suggested. 'Don't lock me out – if you have a lot on your plate, share it with me.'

'You don't need to know – remember how it was before? You want to know all that shit again?'

'Your family? Christopher?' I asked.

'Your mental ex is NOT a problem any more,' he shouted. 'Have you forgotten that I dealt with that for you? Have you forgotten that I'm still paying off that fucking debt?'

'What debt? What do you mean?'

'People don't just disappear with no consequences, Megan. Don't be thick. I needed to call in favours, but the price was higher than I expected. And now ...' he gestured vaguely at Lily. 'People are pissed off. Having a kid with a gorja? It doesn't exactly make me Son of the Year.'

By the time Lily was three months old, the real problems began. As ever, Vic was very tight-lipped about what was happening, but Valerie was always happy to fill me in on details.

It's getting so bad, she told me. *I feel awful for that poor man. He has so many people making demands on him, and I'm terrified that it will push him over. He's been so strong for so long. We only know the tip of the iceberg really, he keeps so much bottled up. I know he could never tell us everything as it would put us in danger but really – when you think of how bad the things we do know are, I wonder what else there is that he can't even speak about? How is that beautiful baby of yours, you lucky thing?*

Valerie changed the subject quickly but it made me think. I knew that I was just someone else making demands on Vic, and I knew I was lucky to have such a perfect little girl, but the fear was building again.

He's been getting threatening messages from Jay once more, Valerie confirmed. *He's getting dragged in, Megan – it's horrible stuff. His dad must be one of the nastiest men ever to walk this planet – I can hardly believe that Vic is his son. They are so twisted and Vic is fighting, fighting all the time for you and Lily.*

That night, I had it out with Vic.

'You need to tell me things, you need to share with me,' I cried. 'We have a baby together – you must know that I'm committed to you, so why not let me carry this burden as well?'

He looked defeated. 'It's too much, Megan. You don't know what they're like.'

'Well, how can I? You tell me nothing and I don't even see anything in the news about it. If they're so lawless, why is it all kept quiet? Why is there such silence?'

'It's because they ARE fucking lawless!' he said, in exasperation. Nothing was ever in the media, but, as Vic explained, that was because it was all gypsy-related. 'No one cares what we do to each other,' he said. 'There's such prejudice – but we can make the most of that; we can conduct our business without the bastards watching us all the time, that's what they don't seem to have cottoned on to. You want to know everything?' he said. 'You have no idea what you're asking, no idea what you're opening up, Megan … but, if that's what you want.'

A couple of days later I found him brooding in the kitchen. Lily was being as tricky as ever, and I must have walked miles round the house that day trying to get her to sleep. The wind was howling and the rain was lashing the windows, so we'd barely got outside apart from school drop-off and pick-up with Ruby. Lily would only sleep if she was on me, and even then she wasn't too keen on me sitting down – she liked me moving constantly or she would scream. I was exhausted, but I could see that Vic was too.

'Has something happened?' I asked.

I could see him work out whether to brush me off as usual, or whether to actually tell me what was going on. 'You wanted to know …' he said, quietly.

'I did! I do!'

'My world, Megan ... there are some things you just have to do.'

'What do you have to do, Vic?'

'There are things I was brought up with that I can't just ignore or throw away. Loyalty, respect – no, actually, disrespect more than that. You haven't a clue what they say about you. I need to fight my ground. Literally.'

His father, Jay, had told Vic that he had to meet him in Liverpool for a fight. It was such a cliché, the sort of thing you see on TV, a bare-knuckle gypsy feud between the feuding generations. But, as Vic explained to me, clichés are clichés for a reason. All the things that I associated with gypsy life were actually true – they did hold grudges, they did obsess about anyone dishonouring their family name, and they did, it would appear, meet each other at dead of night for bare-knuckle brawls. Jay didn't know any other way and Vic explained to me that he had to meet him on those terms. His dad wouldn't listen to reason, so Vic's only hope, the only way to stop the threats in a few days' time, was to do this. It was made clear that if he didn't turn up, then his dad and his associates would be coming to the house to find him.

It all turned out to be quite low key – Vic left without saying anything to me, just kissing Lily on the head and telling her that he loved her. I messaged Valerie but there was nothing coming back, and the next day Vic just turned up at home. He had a black eye and some cuts on his face, but seemed OK.

'Jesus, Vic! Why didn't you get in touch?' I shouted. 'You could have been dead for all I knew! No one was telling me anything!'

'I'll tell you this,' he said. 'I won. I spoke to him in the only language he understands. It's over.'

'What happened?'

'What do you think happened? He wanted to fight – the old man wanted to fight. But I had more to lose and I beat him. He can barely fucking walk and he deserves it.'

I desperately hoped that would be the end of the matter, but it was just the start. For the next few months, things got heavier and heavier with Jay. One time shortly before Christmas, Vic's mum, Isabella, got in touch with him to ask him to come to London to meet her. Vic was over the moon, as his mum had stopped talking to him ever since Willow had badmouthed me to her, but he did have the odd clandestine phone call with her when his dad wasn't around. His mum had said that she would like to meet Lily at some point but Jay would not allow it, and it was even less likely after Vic had beaten him.

'It's over a year since I've seen her, Megan,' he confided. 'She's still my mum, and she's had a rotten life with that bastard. I want to go – and I want her to meet Lily, show her what I've got.'

'Are you sure it's safe?' I asked him. 'For you?'

'It's safe for both of us – it's my mum.'

I couldn't let him take my baby. 'Not Lily,' I said. 'Why don't you go and see how the land lies if you think it's safe to do so, then we can talk about maybe Lily getting to know your mum at a later date.' I hated the thought of my child having anything to do with that family, but I just needed to put it off for the moment and hopefully I could keep her away for ever.

Vic agreed to the plan and seemed really excited as he prepared to meet Isabella. The plan was to go for lunch in London and spend the day together, so, when he didn't come back that night, I wasn't too concerned. I just assumed they'd got on well and he'd stayed over in a hotel.

But he didn't come back the next night either.

As usual, there were no calls, no messages.

As it stretched into the third day, all I got was a quick message from Valerie.

Have you heard from Vic?

No! I replied, so grateful that someone was finally in touch. *He went to London to see his mum but hasn't been back. Did you know he was going?*

There was no reply for a couple of hours, and my fingers were aching with the number of times I typed the same message asking if she was there, did she know anything, could someone tell me what was going on?

Finally, there was a reply.

Megan – it was a trap.

What? Is he OK? Where is he? I asked.

He's on his way back – but he's in a bad way, Valerie informed me. *It was a trap, Megan, a trap! His mum was used as bait to get our poor Vic to London. They took him to a warehouse, tied him to a chair, and pointed a gun at his head. His dad turned and taunted him.*

Taunted him about what? I typed, even though I was pretty sure I knew the answer.

Oh Megan – do you really need to ask? About you. About Lily.

Lily? *Well, they think I'm a gorja whore, but what about Lily? She's Vic's daughter!*

But she's yours too – she's tainted. Megan – Jay said he was going to kill both of you.

Dear God. *Where's Vic now?*

On his way back to you.

How did he escape?

He didn't. Jay let him go. Said it would be sweeter to have him terrified of what was going to happen to those he loved than put him out of his misery there and then.

But Valerie, I wondered, *how do you know all of this?*

He has to leave a trail, Megan, he needs someone to know what's happening just in case the worst comes to the worst.

He says you have enough to deal with but I think you deserve to know.

I didn't know whether knowing was worse or better, to be honest. I was alone with two little girls and there was a death threat against two of us – or was Ruby included too? Did they plan to wipe all of us out? When Vic came back later that day, he was a mess. I had never seen him look so defeated. I tried to hold him, but he pushed me away.

'I know what happened, Valerie told me,' I said.

He just nodded. 'Whatever.'

'Vic – this has to go to the police.'

'The police can't do anything – you know that. They'll either ignore it, fuck it up, or get paid off. I need to fix it, I've always needed to fix it. I was just too soft on them – I couldn't accept what really needed to be done.' He shook his head and took my hands in his. 'Megan, I know I get things wrong, but I'm not doing it because I'm moody or pissed off that I didn't like dinner. I'm scared to get close, I'm scared of what they'll do to you and Lily and Ruby.' So, Ruby was included. 'Who knows what it would be like without all of this hanging over us?'

'Do you think we'll ever find out?'

'I hope so. I really do hope so.'

From this point on, Vic would often disappear for several days at a time, keeping very quiet about what he was doing and where he was going, but I was always given the impression that if he didn't go, then Lily and I were in danger.

Vic's uncle Alan, the one who lived on a piece of land just outside of Liverpool, had always been very close to Vic. According to Vic, Alan was the opposite of his brother – a kind, gentle man, who had lived in his caravan with just his fifteen-year-old daughter, Alesha, ever since his wife had died several years earlier. Vic had stayed with Alan when he had to go up to Liverpool to fight his dad. From a few things Vic said, and an awful lot more Valerie told me, I pieced together some more aspects of the story. Shortly after the fight between Vic and Jay, a Range Rover had pulled onto Alan's land, and as he came out of his caravan the Range Rover's windows were wound down and the poor man was shot in the leg several times. I learned that this was the work of Vic's father, who was furious with Alan for having placed a lot of money on Vic winning the fight between them. It hadn't occurred to me that there would be bets placed on what was going on, and that it would be a public entertainment spectacle for people. I guess I'd thought, when I thought about it at all, that it would just be Vic and his dad, a private event, not some horrible, primitive free-for-all.

Alesha had been there to witness all of this and she'd told Valerie – the collective was often privy to details about Vic's private life so that they could track his movements for work. First, Alan had been taken to hospital in Liverpool, but then transferred to London, where they tried to save his leg. In the end it had to be amputated. Vic was devastated and vowed to get his revenge on Alan's behalf, but all I could think was that someone else was now on his list for taking care of. By early February I'd had enough of all this. Vic was hardly ever there, we had no relationship really, and it seemed to me that if we weren't together most of the problems would go away. All I wanted was a quiet life for me and my daughters, and to be able to concentrate on being a mum, so I told Vic that I wanted him to leave. I realised that this would not happen overnight, but I wanted him to start making plans to live elsewhere. I'd had enough of being stalked and threatened; it had been going on for almost eighteen months now, and it was clear that Vic had no intention of having a normal relationship with me. I didn't want to spend the rest of my life like that.

I didn't really have anyone to confide in. Mum was there for me if I needed her, but I didn't want to reveal the full horror of it. I felt that I'd always been a bit of a disappointment, but if she found out that I was living this horrible, criminal life, who knows how she would respond? I kept a lot from her, putting on a brave face, because I needed her there – I needed to know that, if things got as bad as I thought they might, I could always leave the girls with her, even if it meant surrendering to an awful fate myself.

I knew lots of people but had few real friends; Vic had cut me off as much as he could and he had a jealous streak. Obviously, as we weren't having sex, he hated me being around men and I sometimes wondered whether he even thought back to those horrible emails Christopher had sent, as he would frequently call me insulting names when he was angry. Was there a part of him that secretly believed it all? I found it hard to accept that the charming man I had fallen for had turned into this paranoid, cold bundle of hate.

He'd also started to be horrible to Ruby, which was so different from how he had been when we first got together. I'd loved that he had been so natural with my first-born, never forcing things or trying to act as if he was fantastic, but just taking it all at her pace. Now, he was like a different man. He had no patience with her at all, and she was completely confused. I knew I wasn't imagining it, because my mum, when she visited at weekends, saw it as well and made comments. Ruby was such a sweet little girl and I didn't want her to grow up with someone acting horribly towards her.

His strangeness was even affecting his relationship with Lily. One day, I'd been drawing at the kitchen table with Ruby when I caught a whiff of filled nappy.

'Oof!' I winced. 'Can you change Lily, Vic?'

'No,' came the short response.

'Oh, go on – it probably won't be as bad as it smells,' I tried to joke.

'No,' came the reply again.

I was starting to get a bit cross. I felt as if I was always having to stop doing things with Ruby to look after Lily, as she was so demanding.

'It's only one nappy!' I snapped. 'In fact, I can't think when you last changed one.'

'You can think as long as you like,' he told me. 'I won't be doing it.'

'What? Ever?' I scoffed.

'That's right. Ever.'

I took a deep breath. 'You're telling me that you have suddenly decided that you will never, ever change your own daughter's nappy. Is that right? I'll do them, no matter what, no matter that you're sitting there, twiddling your thumbs, it'll always be my job.'

'That's right.'

'Can I ask why? Can you bless me with the reason?'

'I'm not a nonce,' he spat.

'A nonce?' I scoffed. 'For changing a nappy?'

'That's right – a fucking nonce. I'm not messing round with a kid's arse.'

'What are you talking about? It's the most natural thing in the world! Disgusting, but natural. Why would anyone think you were a pervert for looking after your own kid?'

'Just shut up,' he snapped. 'I'm not doing it. You won't catch me out.'

He stormed out of the room. I made a funny face at Ruby, who must have been wondering what it was all about, and changed Lily myself. He was getting worse, and what was with the paranoid comment 'You won't catch me out'? Did he think I was trying to trick him? It didn't make sense.

None of it made sense. I was living in a world I didn't understand. How could he genuinely think that he would be considered a paedophile if he changed his own daughter's nappy? Were the voices back? Were they feeding him this crap? He hadn't said to me that they were, and I hadn't seen any evidence of it, but, from the little I knew of mental health issues, even I didn't think they could just disappear like that.

The next day I tried to talk to him about it again.

'Vic, I know that Lily must make you think of Zack …' I began.

'There's nothing wrong with Lily,' he interrupted.

'I know that.'

'So, are you saying there's something wrong with me?'

'No, not at all,' I lied. 'But, it was a bit odd yesterday – not being willing to change a dirty nappy for those reasons, well …'

'Whatever,' he said.

It was his stock reply whenever I raised something that he didn't like or didn't want to answer, or if it was just a topic that rattled him a bit. It was like dealing with a stroppy teenager.

'I don't think that's a reasonable response, really, do you?' I said, sounding a bit too much like my mum for my liking. 'You're her dad, Vic. You need to get this sorted out.'

He stared at me. 'Whatever,' he said again, then walked off.

I felt so alone with all of this – there was only Valerie really.

You just need to be patient – he'll come round. You have so much going for you; Lily, the love of a good man. Remember where he came from; remember what he's done for you so far. It'll all work out.

Of course I remembered – I was never allowed to forget.

CHAPTER 8

HAPPY BIRTHDAY

February–May 2011

I think the fact that my thirtieth birthday was coming up was focusing my mind. It seemed like a watershed date and I wished I was in a better place. When things worked between us, they worked well – but the good times were few and far between. We were often total opposites, but that was OK. I was messy, Vic liked to tidy. I'd leave a cup for a week, he was borderline OCD. I wished we could have more of that sort of thing going on, more of the little bits that make you a couple.

There was one thing going on that did seem quite normal – Vic was organising a party for me. He didn't mention any names as it was all to be a surprise, but he did drop plenty of hints about a big-name DJ who would be appearing if he could pull a few strings. There was a room at the back of the house where I kept all of my antiques and things for work, an amazing space with full-length windows and a painted wooden floor.

It was a huge room and he decided to clear it for the event. The kids – mine and everyone else's – would all be able to sleep together while the adults stayed as long as they liked. We moved all of my things into another room, but halfway through Vic told me that it wasn't going to work.

'I've been hearing a few things,' he told me. 'My dad is planning to make this a special birthday for you too. We need to cancel the party, it's just too risky. If they are ever going to do something, it would be too good an opportunity to miss.'

I was incredibly disappointed.

'I'm so sick of this! It seems like we can't have anything without your family sticking their noses in. I just wanted a party – is that too much to ask?'

'Yes, Megan – it is. All of those kids upstairs alone? It's asking for trouble.'

'They wouldn't be alone – you know that I was going to get a babysitter to stay up there with them; she'd have been awake the whole time, that would help, wouldn't it?'

'Are you stupid?' he asked. 'You think a gang of gypsies and contract killers can't get past a teenager? She'd be up on the top floor, where there are loos, where people would be going up and down to get to those loos – she'd hardly know anyone, and it's not as if they'd be walking round with "BAD GUY" tattooed on their foreheads. They could walk right in and get Lily. They could do anything to any or all of the kids if they wanted. But, you know what, if you think that a party for your precious birthday is more important, then go ahead.'

I knew he was right. It was too dangerous.

Valerie agreed: *It's too risky. You need to cancel. They know it's been planned and they are making their plans too. I wouldn't want to be on the receiving end of plans like that. Don't regret this.*

I had to cancel it, there was no choice. I called everyone up and made some excuse about being too tired with Lily, then opted for a meal with a few close friends at the curry place right next door to my house.

The day of my birthday arrived and I really thought that maybe Vic would make some kind of effort to make the day special, but no, that would have been too much to hope for. He stomped past me in the morning in a foul mood. I didn't even get so much as a 'Happy birthday' from him in the morning, then he ended up having a massive go at Ruby for apparently being rude to him. This was unusual – he was mostly very good with her, although I had noticed a few niggles slipping through recently and he was a bit stroppier. He then said that he wasn't going to take Ruby into town to get me a birthday present as planned. She was really disappointed as she'd been looking forward to choosing a gift for me.

'Don't worry, darling,' I told her, 'we'll go into town for lunch together with Lily. You can choose what kind of pizza I have – that'll be my birthday surprise from you!' When we got there, she wanted to buy me a gift too, so that was my thirtieth – Pizza Hut and paying for my own glittery gifts from a six-year-old! I gave her a tenner and stood in the supermarket with my eyes closed while she chose something that I pretended not to see.

My mum and her partner Harry had agreed to come over in the evening and babysit so that I could go for a curry as planned. Although Lily was seven months old, she was still being fully breastfed and I had never left her for an evening out before. It was the first time she had ever been left for long and I knew that she wouldn't sleep for more than forty-five minutes at a time. But Mum said she could cope, so off we went. Vic came to the meal and put a real downer on the whole evening. He sat right next to me and was very grumpy with everyone, refusing to speak to anyone and generally just killing the mood. At the 'party' Vic behaved in a vile way, especially towards me. I wasn't expecting much from him, but he seemed to go out of his way to actually make the whole event as unpleasant as he possibly could. In the evening, with my friends and family there, I could tell that they all thought he was being a complete arsehole. Whatever I asked him, I got the usual response of 'whatever' and I could see my brother looking daggers at him constantly. I was so upset. I think something happened that night; I think I finally saw that it could never work out. If he couldn't even be civil to me on that day, what hope was there? I'll never forget that birthday – but for all the wrong reasons.

As the curry house was actually right next door to where we lived, I could hear Lily going ballistic for me the entire time. If she could have spoken, she'd have been shouting, HOW DARE YOU GO OUT!! GET BACK HERE RIGHT NOW, FEED ME, AND WALK WITH ME ALL NIGHT, MOTHER!! It was patently obvious that she wouldn't settle. Vic was going back and forth trying to calm her down, but it was clear that she just wanted her mum – or that he wasn't making a very good job of it.

At about 11pm we left the restaurant and went back next door so that I could try and get Lily settled, saying to my friends I would meet them in the pub. Lily was in such a hysterical frenzy at being left that it took me almost an hour of lying with her and feeding her to get her to calm down. My mum and Harry left, and I told Vic I was going to the pub as I reckoned I had another forty-five minutes before Lily would wake again so I could maybe get one birthday drink. However, by the time I got there most people had gone home, assuming that I wasn't coming back. My brother Ryan was still sat there, as was my friend Melissa, but they were the only ones who stayed for a last drink before coming back to the house with me.

'Please come back,' I begged them. 'I'm thirty – thirty! I've had a rubbish birthday.' Piling on the guilt, I got them to agree to come back and stay over, but I could tell Ryan would have preferred to spend as little time as possible with Vic. The feeling was mutual.

Ryan was quite drunk but all we did was sit in the living room chatting. He was livid with Vic for being so grumpy and ruining my birthday, and then for just disappearing upstairs to sleep. At least we thought that was what he was doing – but not long after Ryan started badmouthing him Vic appeared silently in the room and, without saying a word, went and sat on his PC in the corner with his headphones on. This was a bit of a pattern of his – he seemed very good at appearing out of nowhere, and I sometimes wondered if he even went to his room. Perhaps he just stayed outside listening and then crept back in?

I was feeling quite tipsy as I wasn't used to drinking, and I knew I was going to get woken up several times during the night by Lily, so I decided to go to bed. By this time it was nearly 3am. I lay under my duvet for a while, unable to get to sleep, with the door open. I finally started to drift off when Vic appeared in my doorway, demanding to know who had just left. I was still a bit drunk and half asleep and I didn't have a clue what he was on about.

'What? What are you on about?' I asked.

'I just heard the front door – who was it? Who left?'

'It must have been Ryan – or Melissa; no one else is here,' I told him, groggily.

'No – listen to me. They're still downstairs – so, who just left? I heard the door. Who was it?'

'Oh God, Vic – not again. Are the girls OK?' I asked.

'They're asleep as far as I know – but …'

He didn't finish the sentence. I was completely freaked out and started to get out of bed. Vic went up the corridor to his room but came back after a few minutes.

'My wallet's gone, Megan – and my phone and my laptop. All gone,' he said. 'Someone's been here. Someone's been in the house.'

I was really scared by now. I went downstairs, where Ryan and Melissa had started to wake up as they'd heard us talking, and told them what was going on. Vic had disappeared out of the kitchen door and seemed to be searching the back yard, which was quite big, with outhouses and sheds.

'He's full of shit,' said Ryan. 'No one was in here – I would have heard them, I'm not that pissed. He's winding you up, Megan – he likes to have you dangling on a string.'

'You've no idea what we've been through,' I told my brother, 'no idea. If Vic thinks there's a threat, he has good reason.'

'Vic likes a drama,' Ryan muttered under his breath. 'Don't believe any of it. He's a bullshitter who treats you like crap. He's an utter fucking weirdo.'

Although I had stood up for Vic, I too found it quite hard to believe that anyone strange had been in, as Maxie hadn't barked and I had been lying with my door open. While Vic was outside, I went up to have a look in his room myself. There was a large holdall bag underneath his window, so I had a look in there. It was full of clothes, on top of which was his laptop – the laptop he said had been stolen. I walked back downstairs, carrying the laptop with me, and told Ryan and Melissa where I had found it. Just then, Vic came back into the house and looked shocked that I had his computer.

'Where did you find that?' he asked.

'It was on top of your clothes in your holdall in your room,' I replied. 'I didn't exactly have to search – it was just lying there.'

He looked really puzzled and went upstairs to his room, reappearing a couple of minutes later and asking me to go upstairs with him. We went into his room and he shut the door.

'Look, I know Ryan thinks I'm full of shit, maybe you do too, but I swear on Lily's life that I didn't pack that bag.'

It didn't make any sense. Someone had come into the house, taken his phone and wallet, packed a bag for him and put his laptop inside? Why would anyone do that? I went over to the bag and had a proper look through it. As I started taking clothes out of the bag I found a piece of paper, a page which had been torn neatly from a book and laid between the layers of clothes. The passage was basically about murder and death, and said something about gold and silver and how hair continues to grow from the body after the soul has left it. It was really creepy. Vic looked really freaked out too. I started to believe that this wasn't him and someone had really been in the house.

'I know who's behind this,' he said. 'I'm going to the phone box.' And off he went.

He came back a few minutes later.

'I was right. It was my dad – well, one of his hench-men, I guess.'

'So, what was the bag packing all about?' I asked.

'He's sending me a message.'

'What message?'

'That it's time to leave.'

Secret messages or not, what terrified me was that someone had managed to get into the house, with my kids in it, and do this. We went back downstairs and Vic went and resumed his search outside. He noticed that by the back door was a shovel from the shed, and there was paint scraped off from the insides of the French door frames on both sides where the shovel had been pushed in between the doors to pop the lock. He noticed that the screws holding the lock mechanism in place had been removed, and he also found two carrier bags in the back yard.

'Why are you bringing rubbish in?' I asked him.

'They're not rubbish, they're evidence,' he replied. 'They would put these over their feet so they didn't leave any wet footprints in the house.'

After very little sleep, the next morning I had a bath, and Vic came into the bathroom as I soaked.

'My dad's not messing around, Megan. The best thing is for me to go, otherwise you and Lily will always be in danger.' We had a long talk about what he was going to do, then he went downstairs. He came back up straight away.

'Did you put the screws back in the door?' he asked.

Obviously, I hadn't – but, somehow, they were in place. I was totally mystified at how that had happened, but Vic said it was just so that he'd know that his dad was still about. Another message, another warning. The screws had still been missing that morning, so it must have happened while I was in the bath, I thought.

That day I was in touch with Valerie several times, and it seemed that Jay was now on a mission to kill Vic and Lily. In the following weeks Vic started spending more and more time away from the house. I had no idea where he was going, but he said it was the best thing to do to keep me and the kids safe. I was left at home on my own, terrified that we were going to be murdered by gypsies, while trying to keep my business going, and looking after the house, the kids (including one who still didn't sleep), the dogs (including Vic's dog that he left behind) and the cats. Vic had assured me that his uncle Alan had arranged, from his hospital bed, for me to be watched constantly to make sure I didn't come to any harm. Apparently I was being followed everywhere I went, and the house was under surveillance the whole time. I was still petrified, though. Protection may very well have been arranged, but I couldn't help fearing that I would be murdered in my own home, with my two girls at my side.

I confided in Valerie a lot, and she was always there, online, for me. I wished I could meet her, but she was either in London, on tour with the collective, or away on holiday with her husband who was in a band. She was really sensitive, always happy to let me sound off, but gently reminding me that Vic had his own problems too.

I'm so sorry to hear all of that, my dear, she said when I told her we were fighting a lot again and that he kept disappearing to 'make plans', thinking his father was finally going to come for us. *Is he still getting counselling? I am wondering if he is on his way to another meltdown – by the way you have described things, I would say so.*

Val would always tell me when she would be back online, and I would hold onto these times as a way of talking things through. We stumbled on for a few months, and he wasn't in touch with Val, who started to get a bit concerned about him. She had been on tour for three months, and was off to Japan for another two, but keen to find out how things were.

I haven't heard from Vic in ages – he just doesn't respond to email/phone, totally and utterly useless. I spoke to Willow and she explained that family stuff had erupted again and that, I know, sends him very withdrawn. I also heard about Uncle Alan – shit, that is heavy, heavy stuff from what I can gather. Jesus – this is one family I am glad and relieved I wasn't born into.

This was all written at 3am, and I would get these messages in the morning, usually after a tricky night with the baby. *I know Vic better than anyone*, she would say – and she was right. I was starting to feel as if I'd had a baby with a stranger. I was crying all the time, at the slightest things, and was an emotional wreck. I revealed all of this to Val, openly admitting how difficult it was to have a relationship with such a troubled man.

Pardon my French but WTF is going on with that man?
she asked. *I have a sneaking suspicion this lies totally on
the plate with his father, damn him. Don't forget, my love,
you have to take his autism and mental health into consideration, plus the fact that – bless him – he is from the biggest
family of hoodlums that I know on this Earth.*

She always brought me back to reality. No matter
how hard I was finding things, Vic had so many more
battles to fight. I just wasn't sure I could be by his side as
he fought them any more. I rarely saw him, but when I
did he told me bits and pieces about his plans.

There would be no going back this time.

He was going to kill his father.

He was planning to murder Jay on 19 April, which
was the anniversary of Zack's death. He told me that if
it all went to plan he would have to disappear for a long
time afterwards. Of course he didn't tell me any details,
other than that it was going to be happening in London.
It seemed that Vic's dad had his own date for killing
Lily, and it was just a case of which was going to happen
first.

'Which of them would you rather?' he asked me,
chillingly.

How could I answer – how could I say those words?
Kill your father, Vic, kill your father – save my baby,
please, save my baby. As a mum, I'd do anything to
protect my girls, so this was the only option, no matter

how conflicted I was about asking him to kill someone for me.

It was decided. I knew I couldn't go to the police, as Vic had told me the gypsies were above the law and I believed him. Not only had I seen it through being with him, but I'd seen it growing up. Living on a farm, we'd had plenty of problems with travellers, not Romany ones but Irish travellers. They used to come and steal so much from us, we had something nicked every week, and the police wouldn't even countenance doing anything. They didn't have the powers and they didn't have the will. Going to the police now would have just put us in the firing line more. I was so alone, I couldn't take any more. I even called the Samaritans one night when I was alone in the house and at breaking point.

'Can you tell me what your confidentiality stance is?' I asked.

'We can't make any promises,' they said. 'If we believe you or someone else is in danger, we can't always keep details of the call confidential.'

I asked again and again, and they just wouldn't promise to keep it to themselves, whatever I told them. I could absolutely see how women who were in abusive relationships would have nowhere to turn. They would be utterly isolated – I know I was. Vic wasn't physically violent to me but I was still living in a situation of domestic abuse, as there was so much psychological abuse. I put the phone down and felt there was no one in the world I could talk to. I sat in the armchair and sobbed until I had no tears left. There was no helpline in existence for people who believed they and their children were going to be murdered by gypsies! To get any outside agency involved meant potentially angering the gypsies and putting ourselves in even more danger. Every avenue was blocked. There was no other way out apart from the one Vic had come up with.

He made his plans, left and it all went quiet.

There was nothing to say, as I wasn't given any information and didn't even hear from Vic for a while. I stood in the kitchen one day and felt as if everything was closing in on me. I wondered how I could function any more – but I did. I just kept going. I had to hold everything together for the kids. I'd become jumpy and on edge. I couldn't sleep at night, I was terrified every time I heard a noise, thinking there was someone lurking there, planning to come into the house. I'd always been quite resourceful and good at solving problems, but I was completely powerless here – there were no easy answers. In fact, I felt as if there were no answers at all. It was my job, my most important job, to protect my kids, but I was at risk of failing at that too. I felt we were sitting ducks, our future in the hands of someone else. When I went to baby groups in town, I'd be making small talk with the other mums feeling like a complete fraud as a million other things went through my mind. I'd be talking about baby milestones and nursery and toys, but all the time I was thinking *we're going to die.*

There was so little information coming through to me, but I did eventually gather from Valerie that everything had gone to plan. Jay wouldn't be bothering us any more.

This will surprise you though, messaged Valerie. *Our Vic wasn't alone – Kat and Willow were there too.*

What? I thought Kat was her dad's biggest fan? How on earth did that happen? I asked.

It's very complicated but, from what I can tell, Jay was the one behind the deaths of Dina and Logan. He did it to punish Kat for stepping out of line and then he framed her for it.

None of this made much sense to me. Kat and Vic didn't get on at all, and it went deeper than the deaths of her two children. I had always had the impression that they had never got on, but now I was being told that they had joined together to get their revenge on their father. Obviously, Kat had known all along that her dad was behind the deaths, but she was closer to the gypsy hierarchy and, while hating him for what he had done, she still had a degree of misplaced family loyalty. On top of that, if her dad was out of the way, she probably thought she could take over his drugs empire. She'd worked for him for so long, and knew the business inside out – I'm sure that was part of her plan.

Vic was now on the run from the police, who had found the body, and from several angry gypsies who were on his dad's side, and was hiding away in his truck, which was being moved from gypsy site to gypsy site. I was still being followed too, both by those who were looking out for me, and those who wanted to get back at Vic. A gang of Spanish gypsies had been sent by his mother to kill him for what he had done to Jay.

I had very little contact with him over the next few months. He told me not to phone him, that we couldn't risk the calls being traced, and that I should wait for him to get in touch. We couldn't have any links at all, so he even had to delete me on Facebook. When I did speak to him it was over MSN on the computer. I was just relieved that the whole drama seemed to be over, for me and the kids at least, and although I felt bad for Vic, who was now living in fear of his life, there wasn't much I could do about that. I did meet up with him a couple of times with the kids, but it was always a flying visit as he was being followed by Spanish gypsies. They were doing so at the urging of his mother, Isabella, who seemed to have taken over her late husband's role as head of the family.

The first time I saw Vic after the murder was when he asked to see the kids. We met at a restaurant in a nearby town. He looked so haggard and drawn, with dark circles under his eyes and obvious weight loss. He couldn't stay long, and, after we'd eaten, he said that he wanted to walk across to the retail park so that he could buy Lily a trike from Mothercare. As we came out of the store, with Vic carrying Lily and me holding the huge box with a trike in it, I noticed a smartly dressed man standing almost directly in front of us.

As we walked past, he spoke to me.

'Excuse me,' he said, perfectly politely. 'Do you know where I could buy a swimming costume for my daughter round here? Useless dad,' he laughed. 'She's nine, we're off on holiday soon and I've forgotten to get her one.'

I pointed back at Mothercare. 'You should be able to get one in there,' I said, 'or there's a big Tesco about five minutes away.'

He thanked me and walked away. It had all happened quickly and seemed perfectly normal, but as soon as the man started to move, Vic hissed at me. 'Walk. Fast.' Carrying Lily, he moved away from the most obvious route back to the car and took us through some bushes around the edge, walking so fast that my chest started to burn. We finally got back to where the car was parked.

'Jesus, Megan,' Vic snarled. 'Are you stupid? Get out of here. Now.' He was visibly rattled but I had no idea what was going on. 'Just go,' he answered me. 'That bloke was one of my dad's mates. There's no kid, no need for a swimming costume. He's onto me and he wanted me to know that he is fully aware of how to get you and my daughter. You need to get out of here now.'

The man had seemed so nice, so ordinary, just a dad doing a bit of shopping for his little girl, but I didn't need to be told twice. I bundled the kids into the car and, telling Vic to be careful, drove away as fast as I could. The whole way home I checked my mirrors, convinced we were being followed. My heart was beating so fast I thought it would burst out of my chest, and even when I couldn't see any cars that seemed to be after us I convinced myself that was just because they were so good at going unnoticed.

Later that night, Valerie was online and I told her what had happened in the car park.

Oh my God, Megan! she exclaimed. *What did he look like? Did he have ginger hair?*

Yes, he did, I typed.

Jesus – that's David. He is about as nasty as they get. He was Jay's right hand man. You had a lucky escape there – our boy did good to get you out.

Really? I asked. *The more I think about it, the more I wonder if Vic got it wrong – maybe it was just a guy asking about swimming costumes for his little girl?*

He doesn't even have kids! Valerie replied. *He would just be playing mind games with Vic, letting him know how close he could get to Lily. I wonder what happened after you left? I hope Vic got out all right.*

I felt guilty that I hadn't even thought about that. This was all far too close for comfort. With Vic in hiding and me still feeling terrified every time I heard so much as a gust of wind outside, I wondered whether he had just traded one horror story for another.

CHAPTER 9

LIVING AGAIN

May–November 2011

It wasn't easy being on my own with the kids, but it was a breeze compared to living with all the stress of the last couple of years. I finally felt like I could breathe again and started to feel as if I could maybe resume my life. I wouldn't have chosen to be a single mum with two kids by two different dads, but there was nothing I could do about that now.

It had been about eighteen months since I'd had sex with anyone, which had been Vic's choice not mine. Although I would have liked to try and find a more meaningful relationship, I knew that wouldn't be an option at the moment as I was tied into the tenancy on the house with Vic for ages. So, I had a one-night stand. I wasn't proud of it, but told myself it genuinely was a one-off, and it was just my desperation for some human contact that had led me to behave that way. I thought it would make me happy but, actually, it just reminded me that I was still in love with Vic and wanted a real relationship with him. I regretted it immediately.

Vic had been gone from the house for about two months, on the run after murdering his father. A few days after I'd had the encounter with someone I barely knew, my mobile started ringing at about 4.30am.

It was Vic's number.

I pressed ignore and tried to go back to sleep.

My phone rang again and again, and I kept ignoring the calls, eventually putting it on silent. Then the land-line started ringing downstairs. I jumped out of bed, worried that it was going to wake the kids up. I knew it would be Vic, so I answered the phone saying, 'What do you want? It's the middle of the night!'

He was like someone possessed. Not shouting, but just coming out with the most evil threats and disgust-ing things. 'You slag! You slut! You fucking whore! How could you do that? How could you do that to me? To us? How could you just jump into bed with some absolute random and throw everything away?' It turned out that, through having had me followed, he knew about the one-night stand I'd had and this seemed to have made him protective – of something that had long gone. I got called every name under the sun, and he made some awful threats.

'You know that I know some nasty people, don't you, Megan?' he snarled. 'If you're so keen on having sex with men you don't even fucking know, maybe I should send them round? Would you like that? Would you like a visit?'

'What the hell are you saying, Vic?' I screamed, shocked that he could be so brutal to me.

'You know exactly what I'm saying,' he replied, calmly.

'I think you're threatening to have me raped, Vic. I think you're telling me that if I try to have a life of my own, you'll be watching me, and if I step over a line you've drawn, you'll send men to my house to gang-rape me. Is that right, Vic? Is that what you're saying to the mother of your child?'

He paused.

'Your words, Miss Henley. Your words, not mine.'

It was clear that he was threatening exactly this – I'd be raped, I'd be killed – but I should have known he wouldn't admit to anything unless he wanted to.

'Why would you say these things? Why would you be so horrible?' I asked, trying to stop the tears from flowing.

'I'm not being horrible,' he said, quietly and calmly. 'It's just, well …'

'Well what?'

'Well … you do have to wonder if Lily wouldn't be a lot better off without her slag of a mother, don't you? Objectively speaking.'

Despite speaking quietly, I knew he was fuming.

'Vic – you've had no interest in me for eighteen months. I'm a grown woman. I'm entitled to a private life.'

'We're all entitled to lots of things, Megan. I'm entitled to not have my reputation ruined by my daughter's whore of a mother being unable to keep her legs shut for any man who looks at her. Those men are probably entitled to live safe, quiet lives. But, you know what? We don't all get what we're entitled to. So, listen to me. I know who he is. I know where he lives. More importantly, I know that he'll be getting a little visit soon from a few boys I've asked to visit him. And I know for certain that when those boys cut his filthy, rotten prick off, then he won't be much use to you, you slag.'

I first picked up that call at about 5.15am, and it took me until 9am to be able to finally calm him down, which only happened when Lily woke up and he could hear her babbling on the phone. I hadn't even been able to get Ruby ready and off to school, as I was too scared to put the phone down while he was making these threats. The upshot was that, for me, moving on wasn't an option, and I might as well just accept that. I had to promise that I would never do anything like that again, and I knew that I would be in big trouble if I did.

Nothing had really changed – Vic had just made sure that I was staying scared. He was still on the run, but started coming back to the house for short visits, no longer than a night at a time, to see Lily. At the end of June, I had been planning to go to Glastonbury Festival, with my girls, as I did every year. Ruby's dad was working there and had a ticket for me, but a few days beforehand I started getting messages from Kat via Valerie on Facebook. This was the first time I had ever had any contact with her, indirect though it was.

You need to know something, she told me. *You need to know that there are some places, some things that just aren't safe for you. You know that there are still gypsies after Vic and, so, they're after your kid too. You're being watched and protected the whole time by people who are on your side – don't be stupid, don't leave that comfort zone. Once you're inside that festival, there's nothing I can do. There's no way I can guarantee your safety as my boys wouldn't be able to control things.*

I had no idea that Kat was involved in looking out for me and the girls. To hear her talk like this gave me some notion of the scale of the surveillance that must be on us. In the end, I decided not to take the risk.

Sensible girl, she replied when I told her. *Maybe you can start making some more smart decisions from now on.*

Her tone wasn't friendly at all but I had to take my support where I found it, not start nit-picking that she didn't want to be my best mate. I was pissed off, though – yet another plan had been ruined by Vic's dramas.

After one of Vic's visits, he was driving back to wherever he was going (he wouldn't tell me where he was staying as it was too risky for me to know), when he phoned me up sounding awful. He said he was at the side of a motorway throwing up blood. I told him he needed to get to a hospital, but he rang off leaving me unconvinced that he would get help. I spoke to Valerie on Facebook that night and she was really worried about him too as he had phoned her around the same time. By the end of the evening the following day, still neither of us had heard from him, and he was unreachable on his phone. We were both very concerned. I thought about ringing around hospitals, but then I thought I would check something first. I knew the password for Vic's personal Facebook account as he had once muttered it under his breath as he had been typing it. I'd never checked up on him in that sort of way before, but now I thought I would look to see if there had been any recent activity on his account – if he had been online in the last day, then he was more than likely fine.

It seemed that he was doing pretty well indeed.

While Valerie and I had been worrying ourselves sick about him, he had been sending dozens of messages to a 21-year-old lap dancer called Rochelle. He had been trying to chat her up, telling her all about his international DJing and how he had a baby called Lily who he saw regularly and that he still got on well with her mum. There was also a very long thread of messages between him and a girl called Viv, where again he was keeping up the pretence that he was still touring with the sound system all over the world. Whereas Rochelle had seemed quite nonplussed by his attention, Viv was lapping it up. There were over 2,000 messages between them, dating right back to the very start of May, just days after he had murdered his father. In these messages he talked about a girl called Sandra. From what I could tell, he'd had a drunken one-night stand with her in June. I was fuming. After all the grief he had given me about sleeping with someone else, it turned out he had been doing exactly the same with at least one person, and attempting to with at least two more! I could also see that all the girls he'd been talking to and seeing were in South Wales, so I knew where he had been. Given that lots of people knew him there it wasn't a very clever place to hide.

All this while he was supposed to be lying very low after murdering his father and was making me terrified in case he was killed too.

All this while he was still giving me guilt trips as I tried to get our sexual relationship back on track.

All this while he told me how awful I was to even be thinking of sex when there was so much going on. I felt this was just too much deception – there were cracks there that I hadn't even imagined.

When I finally got hold of Vic I confronted him with all of this, and he denied everything, even though it was there in black and white. I didn't believe him, so I decided to look Sandra up on Facebook and ask her myself what had gone on between them. I got quite a curt reply from her saying *nothing happened, we were just friends, and what is it to do with you anyway as you're not together anymore?* I was still very suspicious about it all, but Vic wasn't going to admit to anything, nor was she, so I had to drop it.

I didn't see much of Vic that summer, but Valerie kept in touch, and one day she sent me a message which seemed to change everything.

You're very safe now, Megan. I believe Vic when he says that. Now that Jay is dead, Vic's in charge as he's the oldest son. But there is a slight problem.

What's that? I asked.

He needs to marry.

Well, he's never asked – and I don't think we're in quite the right place for it, do you? I replied.

You don't understand – he needs to marry a gypsy girl. Keep the line pure.

Does he never think of me? I'm left to pick up all the pieces. I know it's not his choice but if he was planning this for so long, why did he get me pregnant? I don't get it. At the start, it was definitely him chasing me. I wasn't really up for a relationship as you may remember, I told her.

I do, and I feel guilty for kind of persuading you but he is an amazing man. He is too clever for his own good with music and I just wish he would accept the plaudits for what he can do.

Well, I said sarcastically, *he won't have much time now if he's King of the Gypsies, will he?*

I spoke with Valerie more than I spoke with Vic as he was away most of the time. On one of his brief visits to the house, all of a sudden he burst in to my room, turned the light out and told me not to move.

'What's wrong now?' I asked, feeling that we had been here so many times before.

'Someone's in the yard,' he whispered.

I sighed. 'Again?'

'Don't you dare get so fucking laid back about this!' he hissed. 'This is my kid's fucking life you're not interested in!'

'It's not that I have no interest in it, Vic, she's my baby too, but how many times has this happened? How many times have you told me you've fixed it?'

'Too fucking many – they keep coming back, though, don't they? You should be scared this time, Megan – this is fucking big.'

He went back up to his room then walked back past, down the stairs, carrying something wrapped in a cloth. I lay on my bed, frozen – it felt just like when I was hiding from Christopher all that time ago. I heard a loud bang, then minutes later Vic came back in the house. I got out of bed, still in the dark, and asked him what was going on. We sat in the living room, still in the dark as Vic said not to put any lights on. He was shaking and seemed more upset than I'd ever seen him before about this type of thing.

'Who was it? What happened? Jesus, Vic, what have you done?'

'Megan – it was one of the gypsies from Mum, one of the Spanish ones. He was completely tooled up – he was coming for Lily,' he panted.

'But where is he now? What's going on?'

'Megan – Megan, I had to … I had to …'

'You had to what? What was that bang I heard, Vic?'

He held my hands in his. 'I had to, Megan. I had to shoot him. He was here for Lily and no bastard is going to get my kid.'

'Where is he now?'

'In the back yard, near the gate,' he told me.

'Badly hurt?' I asked.

'What?'

'Is he badly hurt?'

'Of course he's badly fucking hurt – I shot the bastard.'

'How badly? Do we need to call an ambulance?' I queried, wondering how we'd explain matters.

'No – he doesn't need an ambulance. Christ, Megan,' he said, 'don't you get it? I shot him. I SHOT him. He's dead.'

'You shot him?' I repeated stupidly. 'You shot him? Christ, Vic – what do we do now?'

'Don't worry, Kat's coming – she'll take over. She's good at this sort of thing.'

We sat there for about thirty minutes. I couldn't stop shaking but Vic seemed quite calm. I guess he had more experience of this than I did. It beggared belief that this sort of activity could just be normal for some people – and that I was part of that world. The thought hit me so clearly as I waited – I had a child with a killer. My baby's father was a murderer. The shaking got even worse.

'Pull yourself together,' said Vic. 'Don't let me down now, Megan.'

After half an hour or so, I could hear a car pulling up at the back gates, idling for a little while, then driving off with a quick beep.

'Right,' said Vic, 'that's our cue – we've got work to do. Fill a bucket up with hot water and bleach.'

I did as he asked, then followed as he carried it out to the back yard.

'Look,' he said, pointing at the wall. 'That's where the bullet damaged the stone.'

I squinted but couldn't really see anything in the dark. But I did feel a chill at what had happened out

161

there, metres from my girls. What I had just heard as a loud bang was the sound of someone's life being snuffed out to save ours.

Vic poured the bleach and water all over the concrete by the back gate, and swept the area with a broom. After another couple of buckets of bleach he was satisfied that the job was done.

'The body?' I dared to ask.

'Kat's dealt with that – you heard the car; you heard the beep to say her job was done and that we needed to clean up. She doesn't muck about.'

'I thought I might have met her.'

'It's not a fucking social event!' he snapped. 'I killed a man in your yard. You should be counting your lucky fucking stars that my sister has a backbone and has cleaned up that shit.'

I wanted to say it was his shit, not mine – I hadn't asked for any of this, it had all come about because of his crazy family, but I didn't want to rock the boat. Any time I tried to raise it in the next few days, or ask questions about what was happening, I was told, in no uncertain terms, to shut up. Life went on as if it had never happened. This was our normality – threats and death, vigilantes and blood debts. Vic was away a lot, always involved in something, and he kept quiet most of the time. However, he dropped a few comments here and there, plus Valerie was less discreet about things, so

I learned what was going on from her. Over the summer things went from bad to worse. I had been asking her what he was up to, when she revealed something so shocking I could barely process it.

Megan, he's in huge debt.

I'm not surprised, I told her. *We haven't exactly ever been rolling in it.*

I don't mean money, my love, she informed me, *I mean a different sort of debt. After that thing that happened in your yard, the only way for him to get out of matters is to do what the Spanish gypsies want of him. Do you understand?*

I understood that she couldn't come right out and say that he'd killed someone, but I didn't know what he was expected to do to escape their wrath.

Well … the thing he did in the yard? He has to do that again – three times. They'll choose. Once he does, the score will be settled.

What I took from this was that Vic was being forced into becoming a hit man, a contract killer for the Spanish gypsies, as payback for having killed one of theirs.

I was led to believe over the course of the summer that he had completed two of these tasks but, at some point in early July, Vic suffered a terrible injury. He was in London with his cousin, Alan's daughter Alesha, to visit Alan in hospital, where he was still recovering from being shot. They were suddenly set upon by a group of skinheads outside the hospital after evening visiting hours. Alesha managed to get away unhurt, but Vic got attacked with a crowbar. I didn't learn about this attack straight away – after all, Vic was still in hiding and hardly ever at the house or in contact with me. It wasn't until Kat and Willow went to visit him one day in his secret location and found him unconscious in his truck, with vomit all over the place, that they took him to hospital to get him looked at by a doctor. I learned all of this through Valerie on Facebook chat.

When he was being examined, it was discovered that Vic actually had some pretty significant old head injuries. Even he didn't know what had caused them – which was unsurprising, really, given how many fights he'd been in over the years. Someone must have whacked him at some point and the damage had been more severe than he'd realised. Vic was admitted to a private hospital in Lancashire which was paid for by his sister Kat, who seemed to have turned over a new leaf. Kat was now the doting sister, staying with him at all times in hospital, even getting the porters to put an extra bed in his room so he didn't have to be alone. Vic's head was in a bad way. He had a compound fracture, as well as some damage and bleeding to his brain, and he was in hospital for most of the next six months.

Vic never wanted me or Lily to see him in hospital surroundings, so when we travelled north to see him he would arrange to meet us in a nearby coffee shop or park to try and give her some sense of normality with her daddy. On a couple of occasions I offered to book into a nearby hotel so that he could see her for more than two hours at a time, but the doctors became a bit more flexible and said that he could be released for a couple of days at a time as long as he was always back for his next operation. Kat would arrange for a driver, another gypsy, to bring him by car. On one of the week-end visits home, instead of being bandaged, Vic arrived wearing a rugby helmet. The doctors had told him that he had to keep it on to protect his head and, sure enough, he wore it the entire weekend, even when he was in bed. He really was in the wars – he had so many operations to deal with, and often his recovery wasn't as good as the medical team hoped, so visiting would be off the cards for a while.

I was still in limbo – neither in a full relationship nor a single mother – but I cared deeply for Vic and hated to see him go through this. When we were told that the prognosis was even worse than originally thought, my mind had to focus. Valerie and Kat were informed that the doctors would be surprised if he lasted until Christmas.

It was a terrible blow. Despite all he'd put us through, I would never have wished ill on Vic. In fact, I had seen many glimpses of the old him – what I thought of as the real him – when we visited him on his days out from hospital and I had desperately hoped that, when he got well again, he'd be back to that version. Maybe, I told myself, the head injury had messed with his real character, and once the doctors sorted that we could make a new life for ourselves – we could live again.

I had started talking to Kat over Facebook now. She didn't have her own Facebook account but Valerie had given her the password to the Hippy69 one, so I chatted with her through that time. She was not as scary as I thought she might be; her English wasn't great, as she had spent a lot of her life in Spain, and her spelling was terrible, but we seemed to get on OK. I would talk to her a lot online, as she was really bored stuck in hospital with Vic. She was very concerned about her brother and seemed keen to save our relationship, telling me that Vic was still really in love with me and if it weren't for all the opposition he had had from his family over us being together, things would never have turned out the way they did. She kept urging me to hang on in there, because if by some miracle he managed to recover from his injuries, he would need me to be there for him.

Around this time, another puzzling incident occurred. I heard through Valerie that Vic had collapsed and was picked up by an ambulance and taken to hospital. I asked which hospital he was in as I wanted to take Lily to visit him. Valerie said it was the same private hospital where he had been receiving all his surgery and treatment. I queried how an NHS ambulance knew to take him to a private hospital while he was unconscious, and Valerie said that he carried a medical card in his wallet that showed he had private healthcare. The next time he was back I had a look in his wallet for this card, but it wasn't there. I wondered what was going on – things seemed to be getting more and more confusing, but every time I asked for clarification I was just told it was better that I didn't know for my own safety.

Vic had been absent from the house pretty much the whole time since the day he left to go and murder his dad, apart from the odd couple of days here and there. He gave me money towards Lily when he could, but this got more irregular towards the end of the year. It turned out that the Spanish gypsies had somehow managed to clone his bank cards, and would get to his benefits before he did, so he would often be left with no money.

With Vic gone, there was one thing that I had managed to change and that was my support network. I had a friend called Amy who lived near me – she kept me sane a lot of the time. Amy's boyfriend, Brian, lived in Cardiff and he had a single friend called Colin, who often came back with him when he visited Amy. Amy and Brian, for some mad reason, decided it would be a good idea to set me and Colin up with each other – but I wanted nothing to do with it. Even though Vic was hardly ever there, I knew I was still being followed everywhere and I couldn't risk the wrath of Vic, not after the last time I tried to have anything to do with another man. Amy was adamant, though, telling me that I needed to get a life and stop letting Vic control me. At the end of that October, Brian was coming to Sussex to go to a party, and Colin was tagging along. Before the party they were going to Amy's house in Henfield for dinner and she was desperate for me to join them. I knew that Vic would find out and that there was no way he would allow it, so there was no point in even entertaining that idea. To be honest, I wasn't that bothered, as I knew it didn't matter if I liked this Colin or not – getting together with him wouldn't be an option, so it was irrelevant. Just to appease Amy, though, I agreed to pop over to her house that evening before they left for the party for a quick 'hello'.

As time went on, it looked like even doing that was not going to be an option. Earlier that day, for some reason, Vic had gone through a bag of mine that was on top of the washing machine. In one of the pockets he found some condoms. The truth was, I have no idea how long they had been in there for, probably years, but he took this to mean that I was sleeping with someone else, which brought on another of his psycho episodes. It took me all afternoon to calm him down, and I very nearly just called Amy to say I wouldn't be coming over. However, by the evening Vic seemed a bit more stable, so I thought I would risk going over for an hour or so.

I got to Amy's and met Brian and Colin. I was feeling pretty subdued after a day of being verbally attacked by Vic, and told Amy about what had happened. Brian and Colin were listening in and they couldn't believe their ears. I gave them a potted history of what had been happening, obviously omitting all the murders (I'd been threatened with death if I ever repeated any of that to anyone). But I made it clear that I couldn't risk getting on the wrong side of Vic or his family, as that would be the end of me.

They sat open-mouthed and Colin seemed particularly affected by it. He also seemed like a really nice guy. The three of them pleaded with me to go to the party with them, but there was no way I was going to chance it; so, when they left, I got in my car and went home. That night I couldn't stop thinking about Colin – there was something about him I had really liked. I knew I had probably blown it by telling him my situation, but what choice did I have there? I felt so frustrated that Vic had controlled my life to the extent where I was not allowed any happiness, especially when he had no interest in me himself. But then, as he kept reminding me, he had risked his own life several times protecting me and Lily, and was still living in fear of the Spanish gypsies and the police catching up with him, so he made me feel like I owed him.

The next day I woke up still thinking about Colin. Ruby had been at her dad's for the weekend, and I had to pick her up early afternoon. I drove through the village where Amy lived, and on impulse decided to call in. I wanted to see Colin again before they headed back to Cardiff. I knocked on the door, but there was no answer; as I expected, they were all still out cold after the party. I was a bit disappointed, and when Amy called me later on I mentioned that I had come over.

She must have told Colin because, a couple of days later, I received a message on Facebook from him, saying that he would like to see me again. I was really surprised that he was interested in me after hearing about the disaster area that was my life. I decided that I had had enough of Vic controlling me, and I was going to meet up with Colin somehow. I was off on holiday to Florida with my mum and the kids, for two weeks, so I made a vague plan with Colin that I would go to see him in Cardiff soon after I got back. We had a few chats on the phone before I left for Florida, and I found it really easy to talk to him. He was just a little older than me, in a good job, with two kids from his previous relationship, his own house, good looks and a sense of humour. That, for me, was so much normality that I could hardly cope! He was a breath of fresh air. I had deleted the message he sent me on Facebook as soon as I had received it, as I worried that Vic might be looking at my account, and I warned Colin not to send me any more messages on the internet.

It was great being in Florida, far, far away from Vic and the possibility that we were going to be murdered by gypsies at any moment. Vic was staying in the house for a few days while I was away, and then he had to go back to hospital. He had said that he wanted to talk to Lily on MSN while we were away, and I took my laptop with me. However, the wifi connection where we were staying was terrible, it took an age to load anything and there was no chance of being able to use the webcam. I didn't hear from Vic directly while I was there, but I got quite a few irate messages from Kat, claiming that I was deliberately making it awkward for Vic to see Lily. This was the beginning of Kat turning on me, but it certainly wasn't the end. I also heard from Valerie a fair bit, who informed me that Vic's mother had been murdered, although I didn't really get any details from her. This was obviously good news for me, as I presumed that now the hit men that she had employed to try and kill my baby would no longer be trying to do so. Maybe finally all of this was coming to an end and I had a chance of happiness.

I couldn't have been more naïve.

CHAPTER 10

'DO YOU REALLY THINK YOU CAN JUST GO?'

November 2011–February 2012

When we got back to the UK, Vic came to visit, having finished his latest bout of brain surgery in hospital. This time his health seemed to be much improved; he was no longer having to wear the rugby helmet and was not complaining about pain so much. Ruby was going back to school on the Tuesday and I realised that the following day was an inset day. I came up with a master plan – or so I thought. Vic was only there until the end of the week, so my original plan of going to Cardiff to see Colin that weekend wasn't a possibility. But there was another option. I asked Ruby's dad if he would be able to have Ruby that night and the following day. He agreed, and, given that Colin was off work for a couple of days, I decided this was my chance.

That evening, at about 6pm, I got Ruby's bag packed for her dad's and hid a change of clothes for myself in my car. I hadn't given Vic any warning that I was going anywhere, as I knew that he would try to stop it some-how. I made sure that Lily had plenty of food in the house, and announced to Vic that I was going to drop Ruby off then head out. I didn't say anything about where I was going or when I was coming back. I wasn't really sure myself but I knew that, although he would be seething about me having tricked him and going out somewhere he couldn't control, Lily would be fine in his care. All he had to do was get her ready for bed, and put her down, then in the morning give her breakfast and entertain her for a few hours until I got back. She was always happy with him, and although this was the first time I had ever left her with him overnight I was sure he would cope.

So I dropped Ruby off, then headed to Cardiff, stop-ping en route at a supermarket to get changed in the toilets and put some make-up on. I didn't get there until gone 10pm, and as I drove I felt really paranoid that I was being followed by gypsies, but I kept checking my mirrors and I finally decided that I was being daft.

I had a lovely evening with Colin at his home. We had a few drinks and stayed up chatting until 3am; we had so much to say to each other and had a really good laugh. I did sleep with him that night, even though I worried that Vic would find out and I would live to regret it, but there was also part of me that felt giddy from being free, so I thought 'What the hell'!

I set my alarm early in order to get up and head back sharpish in the hope that I could minimise the rage from Vic. When I woke up, all the good feelings of the night before had gone. I felt literally sick with fear. I was actually shaking at the thought of going home. Though I'd had a good time, I couldn't believe I had been so stupid as to put myself in this position. I had no idea what was waiting for me back home, but I knew it wouldn't be good.

My phone battery died while I was driving, so I stopped at a phone box to call Ruby's dad and arrange to meet him on the way to my house. I remember I had my wallet in my hand the whole time, then I threw it into Lily's empty car seat when I got back in the car. Vic had given me his half of the rent money in cash – £475 – the day I'd got back from America, and I was keeping it in my wallet until I could get to the bank to pay it in. I picked Ruby up, then drove straight home, where I parked my car in the secure back yard. I walked into the house expecting all hell to break loose, but although Vic was being very decidedly 'off' with me he didn't ask about where I'd been or even mention the fact that I hadn't come back the night before.

I thought it was all a bit strange that he was being so civilised, but texted Colin to say that I had got home safely and I thought I might have got away with it. Later that day I needed to pop to the local shop for a few things the girls needed, so I went to grab my purse out of the car.

It wasn't in the seat. It was nowhere to be found.

It was dark by now so I got a torch and had a really good look through the car, and it definitely wasn't there.

I couldn't understand it.

I clearly remembered putting it in Lily's seat after I had used the phone box, and I hadn't touched it since. I was baffled, and panicked that I was now going to have to pay Vic's half of the rent out of my own pocket, a tall order with Christmas coming up. But where had I lost it? How could I have lost it? Vic came out while I was looking.

'What are you doing?' he asked.

'I've lost my bloody purse,' I snapped. 'I have no idea how – I knew I threw it into Lily's seat and I've searched all over the car. It's disappeared into thin air!'

'Where were you when you threw it into Lily's car seat?' he asked.

I knew this was a trick to try and get me to tell him where I'd been, so I just said 'a phone box', and he didn't push for any further details.

Despite losing all that money, I went to bed on a bit of a high that I'd had such a great time with Colin, and hadn't been murdered when I got back. That was always a bonus! Just as I was drifting off to sleep around midnight, I heard the landline phone ringing. I could hear Vic talking to someone in his bedroom but couldn't make out the words. The next thing I knew, he came into my room and said, 'You'd better get out of bed. My sister's on her way to see you. She'll be here in twenty minutes. I wouldn't like to be in your shoes, Miss Henley.'

That woke me up and no mistake. If Kat had enough of an issue with me to drive in the middle of the night to come and speak to me, it couldn't be for something pleasant. I was exhausted, having had practically no sleep the night before and then driven back from Cardiff.

'Christ, Vic – stop being so evasive, stop dropping hints. Why does Kat want to see me? What's it about?'

'No idea,' he replied, with a smirk on his face. 'Really, I have no idea. It's between you and my sister. But she's obviously not happy about something.'

'I'd best call the police then,' I countered. 'I'm really not that keen on some psychotic bitch turning up here in the middle of the night to see me if I don't even know why.'

'That would be the most stupid thing you could do. Do you have a death wish, Megan?'

'So, what am I supposed to do? Just sit here and wait for her to come and beat the shit out of me? Or kill me? Or torture me?'

'You'll just have to have it out with her,' he informed me. 'She must have something on you, otherwise she wouldn't be so wound up. The best thing you could do would be to tell me what the hell is going on, and I might be able to step in. I'm promising nothing, but I'll see.'

That wasn't going to happen.

I called Amy and explained what was going on.

'If you get any grief from him or his nutter family, you just give me a call,' she said. 'I'll be there any time of the day or night, it doesn't matter when.'

Vic came back into the room just as I was finishing the call.

'Who are you speaking to?' he asked.

'Amy.'

'Are you grassing me up? Are you being stupid, Megan? Because if you are, your friend will be the one getting hurt in the middle of all this. I'm meeting Kat at the square in town – I'd advise you to think very carefully about what you're doing. If you won't speak to Kat, she'll be fucking furious – so, keep all the lights off and don't move.'

I waited until he had stomped out angrily again, and, locking myself in the bathroom, called Amy back. 'I think I need you here,' I whispered. 'It's going to get pretty nasty.' I was shaking, in my dressing gown, in the dark, as I'd been all too often before.

'Nasty isn't a problem,' she said. 'I'll be as quick as I can.' Ten minutes later she was there, with a wooden rolling pin in her hand.

'You do know this is all bullshit?' were her first words. 'He loves the drama, your Vic, but if he's not making at least half of this up I'd be very surprised.'

The thing was, Amy didn't know everything – I wasn't a grass, no matter what Vic thought. If I could have told her what had really gone on in the past few years she would have seen how terrifying my life was, but I was between a rock and a hard place. Amy stayed with me, and when Vic finally came back, after about half an hour, she laid into him verbally, saying she wasn't going to take any more fucking shit from him when it came to me.

Vic looked furious and I didn't want to risk Amy making things worse, so I told her to leave. 'I'll be fine,' I said. 'Really – thanks for coming, but it's all OK now.' Vic and I sat in the kitchen, and he told me what had happened when he'd gone to the square. He was calmer as soon as Amy left, and I got as much of the story as he was willing to tell. Kat had arrived, with a car full of her 'boys', and they had headed down to the rugby club at the bottom of the recreation ground, where she had laid into him about me. Apparently she had been frothing with rage about what a slag I was and how I needed to be sorted out. Vic had defended me and ended up taking a punch from his sister on his cheekbone, which did look a bit swollen.

'I took one for the team,' he told me, staring right into my eyes.

Kat had now left, and the danger had passed – she had taken it out on Vic, done a lot of shouting, and thrown a few punches. I was obviously grateful to Vic for defending me, and eventually went back to bed. I had been right when I'd thought I was being followed – they seemed to be watching me wherever I went.

Now Kat had seemingly reverted back to her previous nasty self, Vic was alone in his stays in hospital. Luckily it turned out that the StreetBeats health insurance would continue paying for his private treatment as Kat withdrew all offers of financial help and now certainly wasn't watching over him as he slept when he did undergo further operations. It seemed as if her moods could turn on a pin. Vic went back to hospital for a lot of treatment and was gone for the whole of December. By this time he had moved his truck to a farm in another part of Wales, where some friends of his lived. There was a big farmhouse there, where about ten people stayed, and several more were living in trucks or caravans in the grounds outside the house. It wasn't a typical gypsy site; it was a privately rented house and all the tenants, whether they lived there or in vehicles, were in employment and paid rent to the landlord. They were all motivated people, not wasters, many of them artistic. They agreed that Vic could park his truck there in the short term as he was now receiving hospital treatment nearby, and they felt terribly sorry for him after his horrible injuries as well as knowing of his reputation.

During this time I started receiving threatening emails from Kat, in her characteristic pidgin English which it always took me ages to decipher. She really had it in for me for some reason – I could only assume because of Colin. She had also turned on Valerie, which was surprising as they had always been close friends. But the person she really had it in for was Vic. It turned out that the doting sister thing had all been an act, and in actual fact she had paid the skinheads who had attacked him in July to carry out the attack. It was all her doing that he was now in this mess. Her emails raved on and on about how much she hated Vic and wanted him dead, what a good job she had done wrecking his life, that it was her who had been the one to poison our relationship all the way through, and that she wasn't going to stop torturing him until he was dead.

Vic's uncle Alan was furious with Kat when he learned the truth about what had happened.

It's all kicking off, Valerie told me. *This could be the end of it Megan.*

Kat knew that she was being hunted down by gypsies on Alan's side, so she skipped the country back to her house in Bolivia, where she always seemed to go when she needed to hide. However, Alan's associates followed her there and I received the news, via Alan's daughter Alesha, who had now also started talking to me using the Hippy69 Facebook account. She said that Kat had been caught and murdered – it seemed like finally there were no more potential threats to me or Lily. It was almost an anti-climax. I was also given the story in bits and bobs by Valerie, who sounded quite matter-of-fact, as if she was relaying the weather ... but this was the woman who had threatened me and mine for so long – could she really be dead?

All I could hope was that there might be a chance for a normal life with Colin at some point. I told my mum that I had met someone new, and although I hadn't given her even a fraction of the truth about what had been happening with Vic, she could tell that I was much better off without him. She was very keen on the sound of Colin, and agreed to look after Lily for one night just before Christmas. I went to a nearby hotel to meet Colin, who was well aware of the volatile situation with Vic. I stressed that it was vital that Vic didn't find out that I was seeing him, as quite literally my life could be in danger. Colin understood this, and although it must have been horrible for him not being able to phone me or tell anyone about me, almost as if we were sneaking around having an affair, he agreed to play by my rules.

How are you? Valerie asked one day. *Behaving yourself, I hope?*

I couldn't tell her about Colin. She was on Vic's side despite how much she'd shared, so I said I was fine.

Vic really misses Lily you know.

So he should but, this is the truth Val, I really want him to be a dad to her more than anything. I know that they are all above the law, which is lucky as far as Vic is concerned, but the bad things they did were for good reasons. Maybe now he can settle and be a dad to our little girl.

She replied, *I know he will be a good dad for Lily, that is all he wanted to be for Zack after all. In a weird way, I am proud of him.*

Actually, I was too because I respected what he had done for us.

Vic's dad could never really control him, that was the problem, Valerie explained. *He knew Vic had more respect in the community than he did – I think he's more intelligent than all of us put together. He has some sort of sixth sense when it comes to the sort of thing he has to deal with. I sometimes wonder how he knows all the things he does.*

I wonder a lot of things myself! I joked. *I never did find out who the three bodies were.*

Oh Megan, I think you are a little bit behind here. There are five in total – 3 in the UK, 2 in Spain. Vic will have to look over his shoulder for the rest of his life. He has put his life on the line for you and Lily. In my eyes, that is a real man no matter the circumstances.

Vic returned to the house for Christmas, laden with presents for Ruby, Lily and me. He had spent hundreds of pounds on me, which I found really awkward as I had only got him a small gift, and I really didn't want anything from him. He finally seemed to be making a huge effort to make things work between us, but it was all far too late. I spent the day feeling pretty distracted, while he seemed to be the life and soul of Christmas. It had got to the point where I just couldn't bear him anywhere near me. On Boxing Day he left to go to see his family, or what was left of it. That was the last time he ever came to stay at the house.

Amy offered to babysit for New Year's Eve, and again I went to spend the night with Colin, this time in a hotel in Brighton. I was optimistic that 2012 was going to be a good year; I seemed to be getting back to the person I had been before I ever met Vic, and I was near to the end of him having any kind of hold over me. I had made it clear that Vic was welcome to see Lily whenever he wanted, and I'd even said that as she was half his, he could have her anything up to half of the time, although I would find it hard if he really did take her away from me that much. I wasn't sure how this was going to actually pan out, but that was something we could work out once the tenancy on the house finished at the end of January. I couldn't afford to stay there and pay all of the rent on my own, so I had already been looking at other properties. My life was such a strange mix of the mundane and the absolutely absurd.

My friend Caroline and her little girl Madison came to stay at the house in the first few days of January. Caroline had just split up with her partner and they needed somewhere to stay, which was a godsend – with Caroline and Madison there I knew Vic wouldn't come back to the house. I also felt a lot safer not being on my own. We agreed with the landlords, who knew Caroline, that when the tenancy finished at the end of the month we could get a new six-month tenancy with her name on it instead of Vic's. It was a perfect solution for me, as it meant I didn't have to move immediately, and that I was free of Vic a month earlier than expected. Vic had hardly been at the house since April, so I couldn't see why he would have a problem with it.

All of a sudden, shortly after the New Year, I started receiving more vile emails from Kat.

Dead Kat.

Who wasn't so dead after all – and now she wanted revenge. Again.

She was still picking on Valerie and Vic too, clearly obsessed with the fact that I was some kind of whore, who needed her comeuppance. Not only that, but I learned from Valerie that Kat was now back in the UK. Around this time, one morning I found I had several text messages from unknown numbers. They made no sense to me.

Great pic.

You free to meet up later?

Is today a good day for you?

Any spaces this afternoon?

How much?

Are you freelance?

What about 3pm?

What are your boundaries?

I had no idea what was going on.

I got up and checked my emails and saw that during the night my email address had been used to create an account on a sex website. I opened the message and there was a link to the profile. I clicked on it and there was a picture of me and a big banner across the top saying *'Local Slappers'*. My full name, full address and both my phone numbers were at the bottom. I couldn't remove it, as I didn't know the password for the account that had been set up, but I emailed the website to ask that it be removed. Despite that, I received many calls on both of my phones for the next few days asking me all sorts of awful things; thankfully nobody turned up at the house, but I was terrified that they would, especially with the three kids there, my two and now Madison. In an email, Kat admitted that this was all her work, and proudly said that this was only the start of it.

Did u like my little project bitch? She asked. *Plenty more where that came from. Hope you get plenty more clients, you whore.*

What do you mean? I replied. *What are you going to do Kat?*

Spent a lovely time down the poster shop getting a few things printed. Must get busy tomorrow – need to go round all your neighbours, make sure they have one each, so that they know how to access your services ha ha.

I couldn't believe it – she'd had posters printed with the same ad, and soon they were going to be delivered to every house in my street, as well as put on every lamp-post, so everyone knew what I was like. Or what she said I was like. How could someone be so horrible? Why was she attacking me like this? I waited with bated breath to see what would happen, but it all went quiet until a few days later, when I received the news via Valerie that Vic had been arrested. It transpired that Kat had grassed him up for the murders of his dad, his mum and several other people associated with them. There were seven deaths in total. She had told the police everything, omitting her own involvement and that of Willow. Vic had been questioned by the police and released on bail, having to report to the police station every day at 7pm. From a personal point of view, this worried me greatly as Vic was my only protection from Kat and her campaign against me.

Vic phoned me up in a very bad way.

He said that there was no way he was going to wriggle out of this, that the police had loads of stuff on him and he was looking at going to prison for at least twenty years. The police had apparently been unable to do a full interview because of his mental health problems, and he was going to hospital to be assessed by a psychiatrist. He begged me to bring Lily to see him one last time before he was locked away for good. I really had no desire to go and spend any time with him but I felt an obligation. After all, he had only committed all these crimes to protect us.

Caroline said she would look after Ruby for me, and I drove, with my youngest, to the farm where his truck was parked. Vic looked awful, and still had a bandage around his head from his head injury. We went to a nearby pub for some food, then it was time for Vic to go and sign his bail in Cardiff, so I drove him there and waited for him outside the police station. Then we went back to the farm, where Vic showed me around the house and introduced me to some of the people who lived there. Oddly, Vic seemed perfectly capable of standing in the kitchen chatting normally to his friends, despite how he had been earlier and the fact that he was under psychiatric assessment.

Back in his van, he spent pretty much the whole night talking about us getting back together, about how much he loved me and how sorry he was that his family had ruined what we had. I listened politely, but to be honest I had gone past the point of caring. I was happy with Colin, had absolutely no interest in getting back together with Vic, and thought it was a pointless discussion anyway as he was about to get a life sentence.

I didn't hear from Vic for the next six weeks, apart from the odd email. It turned out that he'd had to sell his car and his computer, as all his money was still being drained from his account by the gypsies. He was undergoing all kinds of psychiatric tests to assess whether he was well enough for the police to question him properly and being fed all kinds of anti-psychotic drugs, even being forced to undergo electric shock therapy.

I was continuing to get threats from Kat via email. She kept going on about these posters she'd had printed, and with my birthday drawing near she made it clear that she had a special birthday surprise planned for me. I thought back to my last birthday and wondered how much worse it could all get.

Colin wasn't working and we had planned to go away to a hotel for two nights. Ruby was with her dad and Lily was staying with my friend Jenny and her little girl. We got to the hotel on Friday, and left on Sunday – the day of my birthday. Because of all these threats from Kat about my birthday (again), I thought it probably wasn't a good idea to be at home, so I decided I would go and pick Lily up and go to Colin's house in Cardiff. I was planning to head back home on the Wednesday, when I would get Ruby back.

On the Monday, Colin and I were in his car when I received a phone call from Vic. It seemed that somehow he had managed to wriggle out of the trouble with the police, although he wouldn't really say too much about that. He told me that he had heard about Kat's plans for my birthday and had gone to intercept them. He and two of his associates had gone to a cottage where Kat had been staying, just a couple of miles away from where I lived. There they found a stack of posters advertising my sexual services, just as Kat had talked about. They had also found several home-made bombs, which Kat had been planning to use to blow up my house on the night of my birthday. So he and his friends had 'dealt with' Kat, and six of her 'boys', and he was calling me from a quarry where they were disposing of the bodies.

Even to my brainwashed ears this story sounded unlikely, to say the least.

'Vic,' I said, quite calmly somehow, 'listen to what you're saying. You're telling me your sister was going to blow me and my children up. You've killed your sister. You've killed six of her accomplices. You're now getting rid of their bodies in a quarry. And you're taking the time out to give me a quick ring?'

Colin had been very sceptical of Vic's stories all along, and I think it was him who was making me begin to see that perhaps I shouldn't believe everything he said. But Valerie was always online to back it all up, which really confused me. I didn't know what to believe.

'Are you calling me a liar?' he asked.

I couldn't really answer that as, finally, I think I probably was.

'You have no idea what I've done for you – no idea what I'm still doing for you. I need to be on the move again, Megan, I can never stop. But you … do you really think you can just go? Walk away from all of this? That will never happen.' He told me that he was moving to Inverness, at least for a while. 'I have more debts to pay off – I've had to call in so many fucking favours for this that I'll be paying them off for the rest of my life. I need something from you, though. I need to see Lily one last time.'

It was, I told myself, the least I could do.

CHAPTER 11

CRYSTAL CLEAR

February 2012

I told myself that I would soon be out of this, that Vic was moving, that he would be hundreds of miles away and that, if he was telling the truth, the problem with Kat was over. If it was all a lie – well, the problems were definitely over. At this point Vic still did not know about Colin. Whenever he asked me where I was, I replied vaguely, saying that I had gone to visit a friend in Wales, as I didn't want to be anywhere near my house on my birthday because of Kat. This was probably the wrong thing to say as he replied, 'No problem me seeing my little girl, then.'

I couldn't really say no.

The next afternoon, on Valentine's Day, I took Lily to the farm. Vic insisted that he wanted to keep her overnight, as he had managed to stall the Inverness move until the following day. I was reluctant to leave her, but on the other hand Vic seemed fine in himself.

He had always managed to care for Lily so I said I would come and collect her at noon the following day. I kissed her goodbye and she seemed content with her dad – but on the way to Colin's house I felt worried and nervous about having left them together.

The next morning I had several missed calls on my phone from various friends. I listened to one of the voice-mails, which was from Sue, which said I needed to look at my Facebook. I had a sick feeling of dread, and using Colin's computer I tried to log on to my Facebook account. I couldn't get into it as the password had been changed. Using Colin's account, I looked at my profile and there was the poster that Kat had put on the sex website weeks before, now being used as my profile picture.

The same picture appeared on my wall, and underneath it said, *Hey boys, if you want to know what I like to do when the kids are in bed, age and size immaterial, just give me a call.*

I felt sick.

All of a sudden everything became crystal clear.

He had tricked me into handing over my baby and now he was out to get me.

I jumped in the car and headed for the farm, which was about a fifteen-minute drive from Colin's.

I started to receive texts from Vic, saying that if I wanted Lily back then maybe he could bring her to a certain number.

It was Colin's landline.

So he knew about Colin. He knew everything.

Vic had obviously got Colin's phone number from hacking into my online BT account.

By the time I got to the farm Vic had gone. His truck was locked up. I asked one of the guys who lived there if they knew where he was. He said that Vic had gone out about half an hour before, borrowing a car seat for Lily. He had said he was taking Lily to the park.

The guy gave me directions to the nearest park but there was no sign of Vic when I got there. Immediately, I called the police and reported what had happened. They told me to wait where I was and they would send a car to meet me. It seemed to take forever, and while I was waiting I received a call from Vic.

'Are you listening to me, bitch?' he yelled. 'I'm going to fucking kill you. I'm going to fucking kill your boyfriend. Or maybe I'll just torture the pair of you. I'm keeping Lily, do you hear me? I'm keeping her FOR EVER.'

'Vic, no, listen …'

'No, you listen, YOU SLAG. My kid does not need an ENDLESS FUCKING STREAM of your men coming in and out of her life. She needs me. I need her. You will never see her again, you filthy fucking whore, do you know that yet?'

I tried to reason with him, but it was like he wasn't there. I felt helpless – there was nothing I could do.

I was convinced that that was it. I was never going to see my baby again.

When the police got there they took the details from me, and when they ran his name through the computer nothing came up. This was confusing, as I knew he had recently been on bail, so surely the police would know who he was. I gave them his other name, Steven Cook – the one he used for his false passport as his birth had never been registered.

They found that one.

They found the 'fake' one.

There was absolutely nothing for Vic Morana. 'He' didn't exist, but Steven Cook did – and, interestingly enough, Steven Cook had been arrested for ABH on Zack's mother years ago. An odd thing to happen given that this was meant to be someone who had died when Vic was eighteen. Now, whoever he really was, he had my baby.

The police tried to phone Vic and, like me, got his voicemail. They left him a message and asked him to call them back, which he did. They asked him where he was, but he wouldn't tell them. They passed the phone to me and I tried to stay calm, but he was refusing to make any sense. I can't even remember really what was said during that conversation, as by then I was in such a state. The police told him he need to arrange a time and a place to hand Lily back, which he said he would.

As Vic was on the birth certificate, the police said there was nothing they could do. He was, after all, her dad and he had certain rights – and, I'm sure, to some extent, I was the one who sounded like a raving lunatic. They were only seeing a snapshot of what was going on, whereas I had years of it behind me. All they could offer was to put his number plate on the ANPR camera system, which would hopefully track his movements. They did this while they were still with me, and, pretty quickly, he was 'pinged' about fifty miles away. It was a small bit of information, but nothing that could really be acted on.

'Stay in touch with us,' one of the officers said, 'and, if you hear anything, anything at all, let us know.'

I reluctantly went back to Colin's, and carried on getting abusive texts from Vic throughout the day. He seemed to be enjoying the way that he was stressing me out, which was perfectly in character. The power plays and pulling the strings was what he had always loved, and this was no different for him. For me, however, it was a million times different – he had one of the two people I loved more than anything in the world with him, and I felt completely useless. I had to start trying to be just as clever as him if I wanted my little girl safely back in my arms.

In my texts to Vic I started to make out that I had to get back home as soon as possible as Ruby wasn't well. It wasn't true, but as he had always seemed to care for her I thought maybe thinking she was ill would jolt his conscience a bit. It didn't. He just kept trying to make sure I was dancing to his tune – Ruby wasn't even registering in his thoughts.

Eventually I got a text that suggested we meet.

He agreed to meet me at a pub called The Grey Lady near Cardiff that afternoon.

Make sure there are no cops, he texted. *I'll know if you lie, I'll know if you set something up. And you'll regret it if you do. I'll be able to see you. The pub is on a hill and it's surrounded by moorland – you set a trap and I'll know. I'll see them approaching – I can spot a cop a mile away. I'll be long gone if you even think of bringing a porkie escort with you.*

There was no way I felt safe enough to go to meet him without the police, though, so I called them and they agreed to follow me at a bit of a distance behind, in an unmarked car. I knew it was a risk, but everything was a risk where Vic was concerned. As I drove there, my hands were constantly drumming on the wheel and I had a blinding headache. I didn't know how much more of this I could take. As soon as I got to the pub car park, I realised straight away that I'd been stitched up – there was no sign of Vic or his car. By this time I was frantic, convinced I was never going to see my baby again. The police left and I drove back to Colin's for the night, in pieces. The crazy texts from Vic didn't stop, with him claiming he had been at the pub even though he clearly hadn't been, and then saying he was going to keep Lily for another night. I have no idea where he was with her over this time; he definitely wasn't at any of the places that the police and other people were checking regularly.

I slept so badly that night, if indeed I slept at all. I kept waking up thinking I could hear Lily crying, but it was just my mind playing tricks on me. The next morning the texts resumed; Vic was coming up with crazy stuff now. He seemed to lose his grip on reality more and more throughout the day, and the amount of time he must have spent texting worried me too. Where was Lily while he was sending me all of this nonsense? Was he driving and texting? Was she crying, being ignored, being neglected? He surely couldn't have been looking after her. After negotiating all morning, he finally relented, telling me to go to the Membury service station on the M4.

You can get her from the slip road just before the services. He told me that, off the slip road, there was a building site hidden from public view, and that was where I was to meet him. Understandably, this unnerved me. He could do anything to me, but I also knew it wasn't up for debate. This could be the only chance I would get.

Remember – no pigs, he said, just like the last time. *I get a sniff of them and you'll never see either of us again. Deal off.*

I agreed to everything.

Clever girl, he replied, *because if you mess with me, it'll be three car loads of my family you'll be having a rendezvous with. Understand?*

Again, I said I did.

You'll be being watched. Look out for Audis and a Range Rover, then you'll know just who you're pissing off.

I contacted the police and told them about this new development. They said that all I could do was go along with it and call them if there was any trouble. It seemed like cold comfort, but I went ahead. The original plan had been to meet Vic at 3pm but, as I was about to leave, that got changed to 7pm. There were more hours of sitting around feeling like I was going crazy, and then the really mad texts started. It didn't take long to realise they weren't for me – but they certainly were *about* me.

Give her the kid as planned.

If she doesn't cause any trouble, let her go.

Slightest sign that the pigs are there, take her too.

If she brings that bastard Colin with her, grab him.

Bring him back to base.

He'll get what's due to him.

Remember – don't hurt the kid.

Remember – bring her if there's any problem.

Remember – bring her boyfriend back to base. He's disrespected me. He needs to pay.

I'll be waiting for him – anyone who brings him to me will see just how grateful I am.

There was no way I could take Colin into that. My friend Amy had been with me since Lily had gone missing and she offered to drive there in convoy. Colin wasn't happy, he wasn't scared of Vic and wanted to look after me, but I preferred that we took the texts seriously. We had got them by mistake – we'd be stupid not to act on the information.

I set off, allowing plenty of time to get to the slip road, with Amy following behind. As I got onto the A road that would take me to the motorway, I got a call from Vic to make sure I was on my way. In the background, I could hear Lily saying 'Mama' and it ripped my heart out. I carried on driving through the tears and continued to get all the texts meant for gypsies, confirming that I was being followed by one of them and didn't seem to have any police with me. I was so glad that Colin hadn't come, as it would have been dangerous for him. I was pretty sure Vic wouldn't hurt me.

I was ahead of schedule by about thirty minutes, when another text pinged through.

Bad move, you got the police involved, it said.

No, no, Vic! I replied, frantically trying to text as I drove, not really caring any more about what happened to me. I just needed Lily. My head was spinning – I didn't think that I might crash, I didn't care – it didn't seem to register that, if I did, Lily would be without me for ever. I just needed to know that he wouldn't harm her while she was with him. He was still her dad – he would always be her dad – surely he wouldn't do anything that would hurt his own flesh and blood?

Of course I don't have any police with me! I kept texting – and I was telling the truth, I was alone in the car – but within seconds I started to get another deluge of texts meant for Vic's gypsy friends.

Deal's off.

Bitch has told the cops.

They're all on their way.

Move out, move out now!

Meet me back at base – get the kid back there; I knew we shouldn't trust her.

Feeling sick with worry, I carried on driving the last few miles to what had been the meeting point and sat at the service station for two hours with Amy. The first thing I did was call 999, and spoke to the police, who were pretty unhelpful. They then left a message for Vic, who eventually called them back and told them it was late, Lily was tired, she was safe with her dad and he would bring her back to me, at home, the next day. I felt broken. I didn't want to drive home without Lily, but I was at the mercy of that nutcase and all I had to go on was his word. So, somehow, I drove back. I got home at around midnight. Walking into the house, with her toys and things everywhere, was torture. I looked and felt like a zombie.

The next morning, I found when I logged into my computer that Vic had been busy the previous night, changing the passwords and security information on all of my email accounts, and even my eBay accounts, to the point where I could no longer access any of them. It wasn't enough that he was torturing me by kidnapping my daughter, he had to stick the boot in by sitting up all night doing this to me as well. I could get as far as seeing that the recovery email address used on my email accounts and the login email address for my Facebook account had been changed to that of his supposedly dead sister, the sister he had allegedly murdered a few days before.

The morning passed and I didn't hear from him. His phone was still going through to the answering machine as it had been for the previous three days. I couldn't go on like this – I needed to fight back. He still had my child and he was still trying to ruin my life. I had spent so long doing what he said – no police, no solicitors, he would fix everything. Now, I needed to know just what I was up against but I also wanted him to know that he was facing a fight too. I contacted a legal firm that morning and gave them a rundown of what had happened. They arranged for me to go and see a solicitor that afternoon, a woman called Marianne Spencer, to get the ball rolling in case I needed a court order to get Lily back.

Marianne was tall and dark and serious. I was sure that she was very competent to be in her job, but I also doubted that she had faced anything like this – by the time my story was through, she would probably regret the day I'd ever walked in her office. As I sat there, listening to my own story, wondering at the amazing things I was actually saying, my phone rang. I saw it was the police, so apologising for my manners I answered it.

'We've spoken to Mr Morana,' the officer told me. 'He was warned that this matter is now getting serious, and if he doesn't return Lily to you today, then the matter will be escalated. He has promised to bring Lily to the police station at 6pm.'

'I don't believe it for a second,' I replied. 'He's given me the run-around for three days – he won't stop now; he'll be enjoying it too much.'

'We don't know that, Miss Henley. We have to assume that he will stick to his word, so you need to be here regardless, in case he does bring Lily back.'

It was now after 2pm, and there was little time. I hung up, grabbed my things, apologised again to Marianne and headed home. I threw some clothes for Lily into a bag and arranged for a friend to pick Ruby up from school. Poor Ruby. She had lost her mother somewhere in all of this, and now her sister was gone too. I needed to make it all right, and I would – as soon as I had Lily in my arms again.

Amy, who was such an amazing friend, agreed to drive me and we battled through the Friday rush-hour traffic. I called the police and warned them that there was no way I was going to get there for 6pm, but I was trying as hard as possible.

Just before the time I was meant to be there, they rang me back.

'Mr Morana is here,' I was told.

'With Lily? Do you have Lily?' I screamed, as Amy tried to stay focused on the road.

'Yes, Miss Henley – we have Lily. She is safe and well. She's waiting for you. We are going to make sure Mr Morana does not leave until you get here. I suspect you'd like some answers.'

I hung up in tears. Yes, I wanted answers, but I wanted my baby more.

The last part of the journey seemed to take for ever, and by the time we had found the police station and parked, it was about 7.30pm.

When I got there, I foolishly expected to see Lily immediately, but it wasn't to be. I was told to sit in the waiting area. With Amy at my side, I twiddled my thumbs, stood up, sat down, bit the inside of my cheek, nibbled on the ends of my hair – then finally, finally, finally, she was there!

My baby, my gorgeous little girl, my darling daughter.

In *his* arms.

She was crying her eyes out, and dressed in a dirty Babygro with her feet rammed in her shoes over the Babygro itself. Vic handed her over without a word, then walked away. It was over in seconds, with not a word spoken between us.

I was taken into an interview room. Lily was still howling; she was so upset that it took a good ten to fifteen minutes of me cuddling her before she calmed down.

'Where is he?' I asked. 'Where has he gone? You said you'd keep him so that I could get some answers – well, I want them now!'

The police explained that Vic had written a letter while he was waiting for me, and wanted to speak to me when I'd calmed down if possible so that we could come to some sort of arrangement about his future access to her.

'Access! Access! He stole my child – and he wants access?'

'There's a letter, Miss Henley – you should read it.'

I flattened the scrawled note on the table in front of me and read:

Dear Megan – I am very sorry that I kept Lily for longer than you wanted. I have missed her so much and I just wanted to be with her. I am her father after all, and I want to be a good father. I'm sure you wouldn't deny me that. I lost track of time and then I panicked, thinking I was in trouble. As you know, I have my own demons to fight and I treasure the times when I can just be with my little girl. However, I was so worried that you thought I was keeping her too long and I got scared about what might happen to me. I fucked up. I'm sorry but I'm only human. I hope we can come to some arrangement about me seeing Lily as she means the world to me. I know you are very busy, which is probably why you are late for this meeting, perhaps with your boyfriend or something, but I will always be there and will drop everything for my little girl.

I could have screamed. The only reason I was late was because the actions of that idiot had sent me back home the night before, and now he was dropping nasty little hints about me being 'busy' and with a 'boyfriend' while he laid his worries on thickly.

As I read the letter, which the police had obviously seen before me, I wondered what I would say to Vic. I needn't have wasted any time thinking about it as the police soon told me that he'd already left. He must have worked out for himself that me and him sitting down for a chat about when he could next have Lily wasn't going to happen in this lifetime. The police told me I could leave and gave me a carrier bag with her things in it. There was a receipt in the bottom. It showed that at 6.50pm the previous night Vic had been in a Sainsbury's miles away from the so-called meet-up point, buying wet wipes for Lily (these wipes were in the bag that I got back so I know it was him). This showed that there had never been any intention for him or anyone else to come to meet me that night at that time.

Amy and I headed out to the car with Lily, who had calmed down and seemed very sleepy. I took her back to Colin's and got her changed into some clean pyjamas as soon as we got in. I quickly changed her nappy while she was standing up drinking her milk, putting a clean pull-up on her swiftly and just concentrating on getting her into bed, knowing that the next day we had another drive to get to Sussex and reunite Lily with Ruby.

She had a fitful night, waking in tears several times. The next morning, when I lay her down to do a proper nappy change, I saw in horror that her bottom was bleeding, with huge sores everywhere, and the whole area was red and raw. She was prone to nappy rash when a lot younger but I had never seen anything like that. Vic must have hardly changed her at all during the time he had her. She screamed as I wiped and changed her (and would do so for a month), writhing around in agony. Later that day I noticed that the poor little thing couldn't even sit down without being in pain – she must only have coped in the car seat because she was so exhausted.

I returned to Sussex that day to get back to my other baby. There was huge relief in being together again.

Over the weekend a few things started to fall into place. During the days that Lily had been missing, Colin and some friends of his had been driving around Cardiff speaking to people who knew Vic, trying to build up a picture of what was really happening as well as looking for Lily. He found women who had slept with Vic while he and I had been together, and others that he was still stringing along. He spoke to travellers who laughed in his face when he asked them about Vic the Gypsy King. He found someone who told us to take a closer look at the StreetBeats page and do a Google search of some of the images. We did – and they were photoshopped, every single one. Festivals he had allegedly been to had never existed, awards events had never taken place. Pictures were doctored, superimposed, edited.

Colin investigated all of this for days. He checked in with me constantly, asking for information, getting all the details.

No one had ever met Valerie or Leah or Clare.

No one had ever met Kat or Vic's parents.

There were no records of any of the many deaths and killings.

StreetBeats wasn't registered with the Charity Commission.

Christopher hadn't been behind a vendetta.

This had been Vic all along. Vic and his imagination.

I was stunned. Every time Colin phoned or texted, another little piece of the story fell apart.

Everything was a lie.

CHAPTER 12

WHITE KNIGHTS AND DARK DAYS

February 2012

Although I had spoken online to Valerie or Leah or Clare pretty much every day over the course of the last two and a half years, I had never met them – there had been plans, but they had always fallen through. They were touring, or had their own troubles, or were DJing themselves. There was always an excuse. I suppose it was odd that there had only been online messages, even after I'd had Lily, but I was swept along in thinking that they all had these glamorous lives while I was the dullest of the dull.

I had become so close to Val, I thought I knew her really well. She had become such a good friend and confidante in all the troubles I'd had with Vic and his family, right from the beginning. It was because of her vouching for Vic's good character that I was ever prepared to give him a chance in the first place. She had such a distinctive character, and Vic had pointed her out to me in music videos of other artists, so I even knew what she looked like – or thought I did. He had shown her to me in a promo for Spiral Tribe performing a song called 'Forward the Revolution'. Spiral Tribe was a large collaboration of musicians involved with dance music, and Vic had claimed they were all friends.

I felt so stupid. She was just a random woman in the crowd – and I was just an idiot who had been taken in. As the days and weeks went by, I looked back on everything and saw what Vic had done.

He had set up hundreds of fake FB profiles.

They all looked like fans and friends who had been to gigs, but they were all Vic.

Good liars need to be excellent organisers and he was certainly that – God knows how long it had all taken him – he'd created another world.

There was no Kat, no Dina, no gypsy family.

There had been no initial birthday party – he had just chosen me when I had asked after him and shown that I was a caring person. For him, that made me a gullible fool.

He had sabotaged my car that first time he showed up at the cottage.

He had sent the abusive emails to himself – he was the 'friend' who said I was a liar, a whore and a porn star. He kept sending messages to himself, ramping up the insults, making me more and more vulnerable.

He was lying when he said he knew nothing of computers. He was Martin, the expert who found the viruses and spyware – viruses and spyware which never existed in the first place.

Christopher had never done those things – Vic had beaten him up for nothing and framed him for possession of child pornography.

When I had thought he looked like someone from a film when I first saw him listening to the 'voices', that's exactly what it was. He was acting.

When he said at that point that the voices might tell him to hurt me, that was just another part of the grooming, making me terrified, making me dependent on him for my safety when, in reality, he was the only threat in my life.

When he said that he had a false identity as Steven Cook, he was cleverly blurring the picture in advance, in case I ever discovered his real name was Cook and not Morana.

The fact that Valerie didn't exist, and I had in fact been talking to Vic all along, was downright creepy. I had told her everything that was going on in our relationship – and the one hearing my confidences was him all the time. Everything I told her in secret was ammunition for him. I thought of all the times Val and the others had listened as I revealed details of how badly Vic was behaving, only for them to remind me what a great guy he was, what terrible mental health problems he had to cope with, how he had saved us from his family threats, how highly regarded he was in the music business, how much he raised for charity – lies, lies, lies, all coming from him about him.

Of course, I had also spoken to members of Vic's family though that Facebook account – Kat, Maggie and Logan, all of them nothing more than figments of Vic's imagination. He created all of these characters with the sole purpose of scaring me, then having me see him as my knight in shining armour, when the only threat all along had been him.

As everything fell into place I realised just how clever Vic had been – and just how foolish I was. He was the one who had been threatening me all this time. The man I had loved, the father of my child, had turned my life into some sick, twisted joke for his own amusement. When I had thought Willow was threatening me and my baby – it was him. When I thought he needed me to be considerate despite it all because he had lost his niece Dina – it was all made up.

He was the one who had been telling psychiatrists and counsellors about his mental health problems – it was all self-reported. He had moved around the country so much and always had a reason for lost medical files, and they had all just accepted his acting and put-on ways.

He played everyone. He had played me from the first moment I had looked out for him when 'Dina' was killed due to the negligence of 'Kat' – all figments of his imagination, all deliberate ploys to reel me in.

I had read about things like this.

I had read about women falling for people online who turn out to be married, or penniless, or perverted.

I had watched programmes like 'Catfish' and thought how daft the participants were that they had fallen for such obvious lies.

But I had never thought it would happen to me.

I turned on my laptop and Googled *Catfish – meaning*. The definition was: *lure someone into a relationship by adopting a fictional online persona*. That was me. I'd been lured. *A catfish is someone who pretends to be someone they're not using Facebook or other social media to create false identities, particularly to pursue deceptive online romances.*

I searched a bit more – how had the term come about?

They used to tank cod from Alaska all the way to China. They'd keep them in vats in the ship. By the time the codfish reached China, the flesh was mush and tasteless. So this guy came up with the idea that if you put these cods in these big vats, put some catfish in with them and the catfish will keep the cod agile. And there are those people who are catfish in life. And they keep you on your toes. They keep you guessing, they keep you thinking, they keep you fresh.

That was me. I was the dull, flat fish who had been so lifeless, so ground down by the mundane repetition of my day-to-day life that I had fallen for the one who had pushed me into a life full of activity and threat.

There was some dispute online as to whether the origin of the term was genuine. Some people said that there was never really a market for fresh cod, as it was usually processed before being moved; others said that there was nothing to support the idea that a catfish would be a natural enemy of a cod; and that catfish weren't predators anyway. I wasn't really bothered about any of that. All I could hear from every link was that I was the prey and I had been chosen because my life was so dreary that I would fall for any story just to have a bit of colour in my world.

It may seem incredible that I fell for all this, but the way in which Vic Morana created depth and substance to his stories, the messages from his various characters, the public posts on his Facebook page, the bandages on his injuries, the gunshots being fired in my back yard, and a million other things – it all shows just how much effort he put into ruining my life. The events on the night of my thirtieth birthday are a good example of just how far he was willing to go, with the passage torn out of the book and the screws having been taken from the back door and then replaced.

His stories started off plausible and got more and more extreme as time went on. Also, the fact that he claimed to be a Romany gypsy meant that I was dealing with a culture that I knew nothing about – a very secretive culture that non-gypsies in general have no idea of. It was easy for him to explain anything which didn't make sense as just being the way that gypsies operated. How was I to know any different? It was terrifying living my life believing the things he said about people wanting to hurt me and/or Lily; but the actual reality, that none of this was true, it was all just a massively drawn-out and incredibly intricate way of controlling my life, is even scarier. I doubt very much that he is, or ever has been, a contract killer, but to me someone who likes to believe that they are one has no place in an innocent child's life. I still have no idea why he did any of this; I can only assume that he gets some kind of kick out of it and that it means he is more deranged than any doctor has ever realised.

I have been contacted by other people, women he has lied to in the past, and I know now that I'm not the only one. He keeps reeling them in, making himself younger as time goes by so that he has a chance with younger women too. He told one woman that he had terminal cancer, and during their relationship would get her to drop him off for chemotherapy appointments. He would bravely tell her that he didn't want her to get bogged down in the misery of it all, so she was never allowed into the hospital. The relationship ended when he said that she deserved to live her life without looking after a dying man.

He has a long history of making up fantasy situations to gain attention and sympathy from people. Two of his ex-girlfriends – Jeri and Sandra – gave me a lot of support when they found out what Vic had put me through.

Just wanted to say nice one for trying to let folk know the truth, said Jeri, who knew about the cancer lie. *Have known him for years and years now and had hoped he had sorted out all the bullshit but it seems not. About 12 or so years ago he told everyone he had cancer and a lot of folk were seriously worried about him and it all turned out to be bollocks, shame cos he can be a nice bloke and I seriously do hope that he is OK. Anyway just wanted to say nice one xxx*

It was all falling apart for Vic. He had posted on the Hippy69 page, under another name, that he (Vic) had taken an overdose while in Spain at a festival. This backfired spectacularly.

It was obviously just another attention-seeking effort, but people were getting wise to him. Things were getting out about what had happened with me, and I think the fact that there was a child involved now changed everything. People weren't as willing to indulge him – they were putting two and two together and finally getting four. Several of Vic's long-term staunch supporters, or what he had left of them after the kidnapping episode, came to realise what he was really about, and the Hippy69 FB thread became a place where Vic's former friends revealed an awful lot about what they had come to realise about him.

Vic started it all by saying this, under another false profile identity:

Swedish police found Vic in Malmo at around 11.45pm UK time. According to the police officer who came to the hotel to inform us, Vic had taken an overdose of various drugs. Sorry that is the only information we have at the moment. Family and close friends are been informed by the Swedish authorities.

This was followed by a batch of people asking *WTF has he done now?* before Sandra, one of his ex-girlfriends, blew the whole thing wide open:

There is no StreetBeats, there is no sound system. It's all been proven to be lies. Vic was one of my really good mates and he fooled me too – be aware people, PLEASE! she wrote.

Naturally, Vic couldn't allow that, so he came onto the page pretending to be someone else.

StreetBeats does exist. Vic travelled abroad all the time with them DJing. He used to post up and share new beat mixes he was working on regularly. I really hope he's alright, last time I spoke to him, he wasn't coping very well at all.

This was quite typical of his fake identities. They would back him up, say how talented he was, throw in some concern about how he was managing/coping/feel-ing, and generally try to show that they were a real human with real human feelings for him. I recognised it all too well now.

Sandra did too: *StreetBeats is meant to be a charity – call up the Charities Commission. There's no record of StreetBeats, no charity number. On the page there were no pics of them playing, no pics of the girls etc – anyway, this is all old news and I don't want to rehash bullshit. Believe what you want.*

Back came Vic pretending to be a concerned fan to say, *I just want him to be OK.*

But I don't believe it's even happened, replied Sandra, referring to the alleged overdose. *I'm exhausted with the whole drama.*

'Someone' else came on to say they'd booked the team for a gig in the past and they had turned up. Sandra pointed out that she had been there, only Vic turned up and, if this person remembered what had really happened, Vic was 'a bit shit'! Others joined in to say that all the video clips on the page were dead ends, that they had contacted the Charities Commis-sion and been told there was no such organisation, that images were photoshopped or false. It was all blowing up in his face.

All that was left was for Vic to try and hold on to some of his lies by using his other identities. As Willow, he contacted a woman called Debbie Marshall, who then got in touch with me. She had been a friend of Vic's but, like many other people, had disowned him when all the lies started to surface. She told me that shortly after the suicide report on the Hippy69 page, she received a friend request from his (imaginary) niece Willow. A lot of people had been left confused about what had happened to Vic, including Debbie.

Hi Willow, she replied to the friend request (which was always his favourite way of reeling people in), *I'm a friend of Vic's. Would be grateful for any news on him please? Some people are saying it's all a hoax! Whatever has happened? I hope he's alright.*

Vic couldn't resist replying to that. As Willow, he responded almost immediately, staying in character, with spelling and grammar mistakes throughout:

Why people say that? There sick. Not hoax. Am in Bolivia so news not comin fast. I connect with you when I no more.

The next day, there was a follow-up, still in character:

Yes i now hear my unkel take hevy overdose but he ok for now. Thay put him in asylum for his safety, i hope to talk wit him latar if he is feelin ok thank you my unkel get constant help for is mental health were he live he take many drugs 4 voices he hears etc sumtimes 4 him it is 2 much and he wil do something very stupid like now so the people who say it hoax thay are all wrong they not know what mi unkel has gone through they should just be silent thank you I had to start new fb because my family hak old one it all look very diferent now – Willow

According to Debbie, several other people were friend requested by Willow too while all this was happening. I expect the purpose of this was to try and add some credibility to his latest story. He often altered his style of writing and spelling for the different characters that he created. Shortly after these messages, the Willow profile disappeared from Facebook completely, but it had given Debbie an opportunity to get in touch with me and she told me that she had been in touch with Vic when he had kidnapped Lily. His version of events – and presumably what he told a lot of people – was that he only had her for a couple of hours, not from Tuesday until Friday night. His version had been completely different:

From what I remember, he said he took her to the park and was supposed to meet you later at 6pm or something. You were late turning up to meet her and then you reported her missing. He said he took her to the police station and waited there for you to turn up and you were apparently late there too.

I told Debbie what had really gone on:

I was supposed to get her back at midday, then that morning he hacked my Facebook and advertised me as a hooker all over my profile, and sent me loads of abusive texts. When I went to where he was staying, he'd already done one. I knew he had no intention of giving her back so I called the police straight away. He phoned me and texted me loads, threatening to kill me, and just giving me and the police the run around all day about when he would give her back. Eventually he said he would be at The Grey Lady pub at 6pm so I went up there with the police and he wasn't there, then the next day, same bullshit all day long giving me loads of abuse/lies on the text and wouldn't commit to meeting me anywhere, kept fobbing the police off too. Then eventually he said he would meet me at a service station at 7pm so I drove all the way there and guess what? No Vic, so I phoned the police again. They phoned him and he said he was going to bring her the next day so I had to drive home without my baby.

Debbie didn't seem surprised by what he had done, saying: *Yes, he told me a lot about you, saying you were a whore and you had men coming round all the time when kids were there! I didn't believe that, just put it down to him being jealous you weren't together any more. You must have gone through hell. He told me it was his sister hacking your account most of the time – was that a lie too? Does he have parental rights?*

It always came back to that. And the answer was always the same – yes, as it stood, he did. He was Lily's father, he was named on the birth certificate, albeit in a made-up name; there was no disputing any of that. I wondered if I had a get-out clause in the fact that he hadn't used his real name – but the Registry Office said that, as long as he used the name he had been known as during that time, he hadn't done anything wrong. The fact was, he had rights, and that chilled me to the bone. I told Debbie as much – and also that Kat didn't exist.

Debbie told me that the last thing Vic had said to her was *I fucked up big time*. That was the understatement of his life. He had lost his chance – he could have had a normal life, he could even have got out of all the lies. He could have, at some point, said that it was all over, his family weren't going to bother him again, so let's concentrate on the kids. His need for attention worried me so much – all I wanted was a safe life for my kids, a father who loved them, a happy environment. It all seemed so unlikely, something that would never happen now – but I'd still fight. I'd fight with every part of me for my girls.

CHAPTER 13

TRUST

February 2012

On the Monday following the Friday that I got Lily back I was called by my solicitor to say that we were in court in Worthing that afternoon. I attended court, although I was unable to enter the courtroom as I had Lily with me. She was still unsettled and burst into tears whenever I left the room, so there was no way I could leave her with anyone else. My solicitor came out and informed me that we had been given the two court orders that we wanted, the Prohibited Steps Order and the Non-Molestation Order. I was told that it was rare for the court to grant these orders on an emergency hearing like that, without the other party being there to represent himself, but the overwhelming evidence against him and the obvious gravity of the situation meant that the judge was happy to agree to them.

I was informed that the bailiffs would serve the papers on him the following day.

That morning, I received a letter in the post from Vic. He was trying to get me to agree to let him see Lily, and telling me he was staying at a friend's house and that Lily would be safe there. I knew the papers had not been served on him yet, so before the injunction was in place I took the opportunity to phone him.

I just wanted some kind of explanation as to why he had put me through that nightmare.

He couldn't answer any of it – or chose not to.

I confronted him with what I had found out so far about StreetBeats not existing, as well as everything else being made up, and he just gave his stock answer of 'Whatever'.

He was still asking if he could see Lily. I said that it was all in the hands of the court now, and that it was his own doing. He had brought all this on himself. I had never even hinted that I would make it difficult for him to see Lily in any way, so he had created this whole mess for no reason whatsoever, except to cause me a lot of stress.

That was the last time I ever spoke to Vic Morana.

Or Steven Cook.

A few days later I received a message in my Facebook inbox (I had to set up a new Facebook account as Vic had hacked my other one beyond any way of being able to get back into it). It said: *As we cannot seem to find a working e-mail for you at the moment please accept this note as a letter of intent – if you would like to forward me your full name and address I will be happy to send it by recorded delivery.*

Dear Miss M Henley

It has been bought to my attention, that you are/have been stating false accusations re StreetBeats and StreetBeats Sound System.

Please cease using any slander and libel immediately, and desist from using them in the future.

I have already given notice to our Legal team about your infringement, and reserve the right to do so in future.

I request that any slander/libel be removed from any social networking sites/Newspaper articles etc within 1 hour of receipt of this notice, if they are to be seen after the 1 hour you will give me no choice but to take further action against you. This may incur considerable costs to yourself.

Regards

It was signed by another made-up identity of Vic's – he was still maintaining that StreetBeats did exist, and was obviously trying to scare me out of telling anyone that it didn't. So many other things became crystal clear.

He was always so good at taking one real-life event and building on it for his own purposes, using a mixture of careful planning, inventiveness and reacting to stuff as it happened. I looked back on it all and could see what he had done. When 'Nice Lady' had predicted my pregnancy, it was really just the sort of thing that psychics do – a comment that takes on huge significance when proven correct, but one that would have been forgotten if it had failed to materialise. If he'd been wrong, I'd have thought no more about it. I was brain-washed, and everything snowballed.

I am certain that the money that disappeared from my car on the night that I got back from Colin's house was taken by Vic. There is no other explanation for it not being in my car where I left it, and a few weeks later Vic turned up with expensive Christmas presents for me and my girls, which I realise now I paid for myself.

When he had his mental health assessment – the one where he shouted 'I NEED A POO!' all the time – I had thought it was like some clichéd TV programme, and that is probably where he did indeed get the idea.

The £200 a fortnight he got in royalties? I don't think royalties come fortnightly – but benefits can.

He hadn't been born to a 14-year-old Spanish gypsy girl.

He hadn't learned about computers from 'Martin' – he'd been an expert in them all along.

It also clicked for me where Vic had got so much of his 'material' from – when we were together in the early days, he would tell me stories about his childhood as a gypsy. I then came across the book *Gypsy Boy* and read it to try and get a bit of an insight into his life, and some of the stories were uncannily similar. I knew Vic wouldn't be able to read the book because of his synaesthesia, but I offered to read it out loud to him because I thought he would find the links really interesting. He didn't want me to. I now realise he had already read the book and that a lot of the stories about his past were based on it.

I found out later from his medical files that were disclosed in court that the scars on his hands, which he said came about through voices telling him to hurt himself, were actually tattoo removals.

He didn't have epilepsy or asthma or synaesthesia or autism – he never took medication for anything, and they are not conditions you can selectively choose to suffer from when it suits you.

Christopher had just taken the break-up badly when it happened; he didn't stalk me or any of that.

When Vic had 'been on the run' from the police and gypsies, he'd actually been living with Sandra, and she can confirm that.

He was never in hospital with a head injury – he was just sleeping around and keeping other women on the go.

The bang that I thought was a gunshot when he killed an intruder? A car backfiring.

The car with Kat in it that came to collect the body? A taxi he ordered that gave up after a while.

It could all be explained away.

But what couldn't be explained away was how it took its toll on me. The effect on my life has been massive. I'll never recover from the psychological abuse – I'm always looking over my shoulder, to this day. To live in the constant state of fear that he kept me in was awful. The amount of times I cuddled Lily as a baby wondering if that was going to be the last cuddle I ever had with her – no mother should have to go through that. For months I truly believed that I was being followed, by both goodies and baddies, everywhere I went. There were periods when I was literally unable to function through the stress and worry, I would be too distracted to be able to interact with my children, and even just providing basic care for them was a struggle. I am so angry that he stole that time from me and I will never get it back. Even throughout my pregnancy, when he should have been supporting me, he was creating all these lies to scare me and stress me out, for absolutely no reason. To this day I have nightmares about Vic and I am constantly on edge because of him. I have recently been prescribed anti-depressants, and there's no amount of counselling in the world that could bring me back to my old self.

In October 2012 my lawyers applied for Vic Morana to have no contact with our daughter whatsoever. They requested: that a Residence Order was granted in my favour; that a No Contact Order was served on him; that a ruling under the Children Act 1989 was enforced preventing future contact; and that his parental responsibility was discharged. It was a huge list of very restrictive requests, but my team told me they believed it was necessary 'to provide you with all legal means necessary to protect Lily from abduction and emotional abuse by Mr Morana'. It was stated that 'any contact between Lily and Mr Morana will place her at risk emotionally both now and in the future [...] Mr Morana could use his parental responsibility to continue to assert control and emotionally abuse you and Lily.' I was still scared that the courts would say Vic's needs as a father were more important than my fear he would steal my baby.

The team preparing a report for the court conducted a full risk analysis of the situation; they interviewed Vic as well as me, Lily and Ruby; they spoke to teachers at the girls' schools; they read all the psychiatric reports and files on Vic, and attended all the enquiries that were still going on relating to the case. They focused on the fact that Vic had refused to return Lily when he had direct contact. In their words, this had placed her at risk of emotional harm. All of Vic's claims about his own health and conditions were revealed as questionable – as he was the only one who had claimed they existed in the first place. The team noted that he had what were described as 'significant' mental health problems (self-reported); he had attempted suicide twice (self-reported) and had dissociative episodes (self-reported and a diagnosis based on fabricated information given to a psychiatrist by Vic); that he heard voices which told him to do things (again, self-reported); and that he had physically assaulted an ex-partner and had a history of domestic violence. The cracks in the system were obvious – all it took was for one 'expert' to believe someone once, and it all went on a file as 'fact' even though there was no evidence other than self-reported stories.

I showed them all of the messages from other women he had duped and thousands from my FB account. What really worried me wasn't just Vic's fixation with me as a whore and his total inability to face up to his actions and be honest about what happened, but what it would mean for Lily. Potentially – most likely – he would be portraying me this way to my daughter and filling her head with all sorts of other nonsense, as he did with everybody. It would be so confusing for her and very damaging for our relationship, as well as her emotional health.

The team investigating what fate awaited me and Lily concluded that Vic had emotionally and psychologically abused me in a campaign so extreme it was hard to imagine. The court advisor said the case was 'the most extreme I have ever worked with'; he agreed that

Vic had 'lied and fabricated a world of violence, murder and fear in which to control Megan and cause her extreme suffering, believing herself and her children were at risk of being murdered'.

I wonder every day why he selected me when I'd done nothing to hurt him. That's been the hardest thing of all – when did he decide I was the perfect victim?

CHAPTER 14

BETTER TIMES

December 2011–April 2014

Colin and I had got together properly in December 2011 and were engaged in a flurry of romance. He had seen what Vic had done and he picked me up, carried me away from it all, and was my hero. When Lily was missing, he was the one who was tooled up with all his mates to find Vic – he had gone above and beyond the call of duty, and I loved him for it. I knew that he was quite a controlling person, but I saw no issue in that. He was my new white knight – and that's exactly what he wanted to be.

Looking back, I hate some of the things he did. He believed that children should know how hard life would be. With Lily, he would throw her up in the air and she'd find it funny for a bit, but he'd carry on doing it even when she got scared.

'What the hell are you doing?' I'd ask.

'Go away!' he'd snap, but I never let it carry on. I should have seen it as a warning sign, but I was too blinded by the notion that he was a good guy – and I desperately needed one of those.

He was never up for any sort of compromise and he had a real victim complex. It wasn't apparent to begin with, but it soon became clear that he had this notion that people were punishing him, that they were out to get him. It was all in his head. Yet again, I didn't see it.

Colin and I had known each other for ten months before I moved to Cardiff in 2012. We had been seeing each other every week, but one of us needed to make the move and it made sense for it to be me for a number of reasons, even though it broke my heart leaving all my friends and family. Things were brilliant between us before I moved and there was nothing to suggest this relationship wouldn't be a keeper. By this time Ruby was eight, and Lily two. It was a fresh start for me and the girls, far enough away from Vic that there was no way we could bump into him, but also with the potential to travel to family and friends when we wanted to. Colin had a seven-year-old daughter, called Heather, from a previous relationship, and a son of twelve, called Rory. When they were both there, it was a busy, frantic houseful, but I loved the feeling of security from such a huge family. The only thing that was a blip in my life was the terrible tooth pain I was suffering.

I went to the dentist, not realising that a filling had fallen out a while ago. The dentist warned me that it wasn't looking too good and that even another filling might cause me trouble. It was agony for a few weeks and, when I went back, I was told that an extraction would be for the best. By the time I got home it was agony again, even though there was no tooth there. I'd never known pain like it; childbirth was a breeze compared to this! I went to an emergency dentist and it turned out that a wisdom tooth at the back had rotted and that was where the pain was. The tooth that had been ripped out had actually been fine. However, the emergency dentist wasn't willing to extract a wisdom tooth, it was too big a procedure, and I was told it was a two-month wait in Cardiff to even get a dentist to look at it on the NHS. It went on for weeks; eventually I had to go elsewhere for treatment. Colin had been going round his friends, getting any leftover prescription painkillers they might have lying around, so I did feel completely off my head on things like Tramadol and liquid morphine for all of that time.

That lasted for a month. Every day, I was either in agony or completely out of it on medication – it shows just how awful I felt that I even thought that other people's spare tablets were a good idea! On top of awful weather, that's pretty much all I remember of that summer; it wasn't the idyllic time I'd planned for the girls, but we got through, at least managing to spend time together and going to the beach a lot.

Finally, I managed to get an appointment and the tooth was removed just a few days before Colin's birthday. For those few days I felt as if life was just as it was meant to be. We lived in a gorgeous place, Vic was out of our lives (as far as he could be), and my tooth wasn't making me want to kill someone!

Then I realised my period was late.

To be honest, we hadn't been having much sex, I was in too much pain. On top of that, I was on the pill and there hadn't been any times when I'd forgotten to take it. I bought a pregnancy test and rushed home. If I was pregnant, I was late, so it wouldn't matter what time of day I did it. Leaving the girls to watch a DVD, I went into the loo and told myself I was being ridiculous. There was virtually no chance of it being positive and I was getting myself in a flap about nothing.

I sat on the edge of the bath and looked at the timer on my phone. I didn't really need to bother as the second line came up within seconds.

I was pregnant.

I had no idea why the pill hadn't worked, but I was pregnant.

I told Colin as soon as he came in.

'We'll just have to deal with it,' I said. 'It's happened and that's that.'

'I *can't* deal with it!' he snapped. He was about to start a new job, covering someone who was on maternity leave, and he wouldn't be entitled to any time off himself. We worked out the date and it would actually be at the worst possible time of year for his work, the busiest and most demanding time. The house was only a three-bedroomed one, and Colin's daughter was there half of the time, his son every so often, and my two girls. 'There just isn't the space,' he told me. 'It's the worst time possible – and you've been taking medication for weeks. Wouldn't there be a problem anyway?'

My heart sank. Although it hadn't been planned, I would have happily had another baby. My girls were my world, and another baby would grab my heart in just the same way. I don't think we stopped arguing from the second I told him about the test. He kicked off about the slightest thing, was completely unsupportive, and made it quite clear that it was all my fault.

It didn't matter how small the conflict or how unreasonable his view was, he'd make a fight out of it. Heather had an activity class on Wednesdays, and we looked after her every second week. Before I moved in, we decided that, on the Wednesday we had Heather, I would need to take her to her class for 4.45pm. So that would mean picking them all up from school – about a twenty-minute drive from where we lived – hanging around at home for an hour, making sure she got changed, then driving her to her class and dropping her off (again, twenty minutes or so to get there). I had no problem at all with that; in fact, I was more than happy to help out. However, shortly after I found out I was pregnant, Colin dropped it on me that he would never be able to help out. Every Wednesday I would have to pick the kids up from school, drive home, drive back into town an hour later, find somewhere to park and pay for it (which was extortionate in Cardiff), then hang around with my two kids for an hour. Lily wasn't exactly easy at that stage (not that she'd ever been), so waiting while Heather did her class would leave them really bored. I'd have to watch Lily like a hawk as there was an automatic door leading directly onto a very busy main road.

When I suggested to Colin that he could maybe contact the centre and ask if it was possible to change her day to one where he would be able to grab her on the way home, which would mean I would just have to drop her off, he went crazy.

'Why do you never help me out?' he screamed. 'Why is everything always about you? You never help me out! Ever! You useless fucking slut!'

'Slut?' I shouted back. 'Where did that come from? I ask you to help me take your daughter to her class, and you decide I'm a slut? How do you work that out?'

I tried to point out that I was more than happy to collect Heather from school, get her ready for her club and drive her to it, but if there was any way around me having to hang around waiting with the kids then that would be much better (any other day of the week would be fine as it was only Wednesdays he worked late, and the club ran every day). But he was having none of it – apparently I was the most selfish cow ever to walk the planet and did nothing but think of myself.

It didn't stop. Every time I questioned him, or suggested that he had anger issues, he would just roar, 'I AM A RESPONSIBLE MAN WITH A RESPONSIBLE JOB!' and deny that he had a problem at all. It was absolutely bizarre, and I started to question whether he actually resented me being there in the first place. There were red flags everywhere and I suddenly had a lot more sympathy with Heather's mother, who had refused to communicate with Colin other than by text for quite some time.

We had only been together for ten months by that stage. My immediate thought was that I needed to look at all the warning signs and run, go home, go back – but how? I had no money at all, no house, no safety net, but it seemed like the only way. I also wondered what would happen if I had the baby. Was a permanent link to a man like this such a good idea?

I was confused, but I wasn't stupid. I knew that my relationship with Vic had left me vulnerable, and I didn't want to make the same mistakes twice. Colin had been charming, he was educated, he had taken all of us on – but it had changed very, very quickly. He was starting to get a bit shouty with Lily, even when she was only doing normal toddler things, and that worried Ruby. She had even said recently that she wanted to go and live with her dad, which I would never want her to do – so, something had to change.

'Colin, we need to talk about this,' I told him, when he got in from work. I laid out all of my worries and concerns. 'I can't bring the girls up in a house where they feel unsettled, I just can't.'

'Don't worry,' he said. 'I'll make it easy for you. We're finished.'

With that, he stood up and left the room.

I was in shock but knew that I needed to act. Having been left on my own before, I was very aware of how difficult it would be with another new baby. I was also still reeling with everything Vic had done, and the court case had left plenty of scars. I needed to be decisive, though; I needed to do what was right for my girls.

I spoke to Ruby's school and let them know we would be moving, I rang my mum in Kent to ask if we could come and stay with her for a bit, and I made an appointment to discuss a termination. It was all moving so fast – just when I thought I might get my happy ending, another nightmare was in front of me.

I went to the clinic alone.

I sat through all of the advice and counselling alone.

I lay there while I had an intrusive, uncomfortable internal scan and had no one to help me through it.

I caught a glimpse of the picture and thought, *That's the only time I'll see my baby.*

I told them about the situation and about my girls and about the fact that I felt like the most stupid, gullible, naïve person in the world, then I made the decision to book in for an abortion a few days later.

Alone.

I had a week to wait until the termination, and I was told that I wouldn't be able to drive for twenty-four hours afterwards, so I wouldn't be able to get away from Colin as quickly as I wanted now that the decision had been made.

'Where have you been?' he asked me when I walked in, even though he knew the answer.

'Clinic. You know that,' I answered, wearily.

'Right. So, what happened? All sorted?'

'Next Tuesday,' I confirmed. 'Can you look after the girls, as I won't be able to drive?'

'Oh, for fuck's sake! Are you joking?' he shouted, the anger rising up immediately. 'I can't just take time off like that, just because you can't bloody cope. What do you think is going to happen? Why do you think everyone can just clear up your mess all of the time?'

'Stop shouting at me, Colin, please stop shouting,' I begged. It was as if he thought I was extending the misery out of choice. Eventually, finally, he did stop shouting – when he'd run out of anger, not because I'd asked him to.

'When are you leaving then?' he asked.

'What?' I stammered. 'For where?'

'Here. When are you packing your bags?'

I took a deep breath. 'I get the abortion on Tuesday. I can't drive for twenty-four hours. I can leave on Thursday next week.'

'Good. Good.'

That was it.

He walked off and I staggered through the next week. I'd booked in for a general anaesthetic (which was why I couldn't drive straight away). Somehow, I'd thought that would be easier, but there wasn't any option which would be easy really.

I cried a million tears for that baby.

And I cried them alone too.

My mum panicked a bit when I told her I was pregnant, but as soon as I said I'd booked an abortion she was much more supportive. On the one hand, I was so glad that she was going to be there for me, on the other, my hand fluttered to my belly and I thought, *I'm so sorry, baby, I really don't want to do this.*

Mum said we could all stay with her in Ashford until I found a place, and that she would go and look at houses for us. It was what I needed – or at least part of what I needed. What I wanted more than anything was for it all to be over. I was finding it so hard to come to terms with my own decision; I'd go to bed thinking I was 99 per cent sure I was doing the right thing, then I'd dream about the baby and wake up in a state again.

The days went by and, naturally, Monday evening arrived. I sat upstairs in the bedroom after reading bedtime stories to the girls and my mind started wandering, thinking about what the next day held. There was obviously no hope for my relationship with Colin – and I couldn't risk holding on to something that might never happen while the pregnancy progressed. He was too unpredictable, too unstable for me to risk it.

That night, the night before I was booked in, he came into the kitchen while I was making dinner for the kids. He sat at the table while I chopped veg and poured fruit juice.

'You know, Megan,' he began, 'I've been thinking about this. Tomorrow. What you're planning to do.'

'What I'm planning to do?' I repeated, already knowing that he was going to say something that would show he was taking no responsibility for anything.

'Mmmm … half of me maybe … well, perhaps you shouldn't do it.'

I could see exactly what he was doing. He thought no such thing, but he did want to appease his own guilt for future reference.

'Are you joking?' I asked.

'No, not at all.'

'So, what do you suggest we do, given that it was you who said you'd "make it easy" for me and separate?'

'Well, maybe that was hasty too. There are a few solutions really – you could move back home.'

'I don't have a home any more – I gave it up to live with you,' I reminded him.

'Well, stay with your mum or friends or …' he waved his hand around airily, as if working out where I could stay was not really that important. 'And you could have your baby.'

'Our baby,' I asserted.

'Yes, quite. So, you could move in with your mum or a friend, or maybe get a house if you could afford it, get the girls sorted, have the baby and, when I had time, I could pop down once or twice a month at weekends. What do you think?'

I took a deep breath – better than killing him really.

'I think – that I'm not the most naïve one in this relationship after all.'

'Well, don't say I didn't try,' he snarled, stomping off to the lounge.

I felt pretty crap that evening and cried a lot. I hoped that Colin wouldn't try to come up with any more 'solutions' as they were clearly just making things even worse.

My mum arrived in the morning and took me to the clinic in a state of detached shock. I couldn't really think about what was happening or I would have never gone through with it. I signed in, spoke some words to some people that I can't really remember, and somehow found myself dressed in a gown for theatre. I kept it all together until I was lying on the trolley and about to be wheeled in.

'Just a little scratch,' said the nurse as she went to put the needle in, and I screamed. The tears were flooding from me and I was shaking. They were great about it; naturally, they had to check that I was doing what I wanted to. I wasn't, though – my heart was breaking. If things could have been different with Colin, I wouldn't have been there. I didn't feel like I had any options, but I managed to calm down enough for them to administer the anaesthetic.

Then it was done.

I woke up ten minutes after it was over in the operating theatre with four other women on trollies alongside me. It hit me that their job was to give abortions in batches of five. In recovery, I was shell-shocked until they said I could leave.

The guilt I expected didn't come.

I had moments of sadness, but I believed that what I did was the best thing for my kids and for me. It was the only real option. Sometimes you just have to do what you have to do. I was sure that there would be moments in the future when I would find it hard to think about, but right then I was feeling relieved and positive and hopeful that better things were around the corner.

On the Wednesday, I woke up feeling a lot better. I was still slightly woozy and emotional but relieved that I'd got off the seesaw of decision-making. I was proud that I had made a choice and stuck to it. As the day went on, I was less emotional than I had expected to be, and focused on the girls, trying to count my blessings. As soon as I could drive, we'd be on our way, on to a new chapter, a chapter without a man messing things up. I managed to hold everything together until I went to bed that night. The anaesthetic had pretty much worn off and we had a long day ahead of us once dawn broke. The tears started to fall, which was only natural really, and I sensed Colin's presence in the doorway.

'Here come the waterworks,' he said. 'Well, I *tried* to talk you out of it.'

The only thing that really surprised me was that he used that line within twenty-four hours; I thought he might be able to hold out a bit longer before trying to make me feel bad and himself out to be the good guy.

Colin's words and ploys didn't matter – they did make things harder, as they were a distraction, but they couldn't change my ultimate plan. I was going to stay with my mum and her partner until I found somewhere for me and the girls, which would hopefully be soon, as quite a few people were looking on my behalf. He ramped things up a bit as I was packing by telling me, 'You killed my baby when all you had to do was make a bit of effort to change,' but I could see right through him. I only had to get through a bit more of this hell before I was out of there.

His next approach was to be over me like a rash while I tried to get things organised. 'Just once for old time's sake,' he pleaded, presumably panicking that he'd never find anyone stupid enough to sleep with him ever again. I looked at him incredulously. Less than forty-eight hours after an abortion, he was pestering me for sex. When I made it clear that there was absolutely no chance of that happening, he then moved on to the usual 'slut' comments. As I took things from the wardrobe and packed them in a case, he asked which dress I'd be wearing next time I was out on the pull.

It was vile.

I'd had a termination the day before, and Colin hadn't said a single thing that wasn't about making him feel better or me feel worse.

It had the opposite effect to the one he intended, though. I actually felt fine. I was amazed that I wasn't in complete bits, given that I never ever thought I could go through with a termination and I had been so conflicted in the days leading up to it.

My mum and her partner were so lovely as soon as we got to her house. We all unloaded the hired van in a warm glow – the girls sensed that we were out of something bad, and Mum was happy that I'd chosen the right path this time. We laughed and worked until midnight, then I had the best night's sleep I'd had for months. The bed was comfy and cosy; Mum was indulging me at every opportunity, and the girls came in to bounce with me as soon as they woke up. Mum cooked a huge fry-up for breakfast and then told me to soak in the bath for as long as I wanted. I did. I felt safe.

The rest of that week was hectic. I had school to sort out for Ruby, and nursery for Lily. I needed a new solicitor as things were still rumbling on with Vic, and I decided that the three of us needed a treat. I didn't have the cash for a month in the Seychelles, but I sorted out five days at Butlins while Ruby's school application was being processed! Not exactly luxury, but it would suit us just fine.

The only fly in the ointment came via text. Colin had started messaging me as soon as I left – saying how much he loved me and how weird the house felt with all of us gone. He was still suggesting that we see each other a couple of weekends a month but there could be no future in that, so there was no point in even discussing it. He had killed our relationship and he would just have to accept that.

It was so nice to be in a calm environment and not be treading on eggshells any more. Ruby and Lily dealt with the change really well and I was so glad I'd got them out of Cardiff. The house hunting was successful too, and after five weeks or so living with my mum we moved into our new home at Boughton Lees, about four miles away. I decided it was best to stay near Mum, even though it meant I would be over an hour's drive away from my friends, because she was offering to help me out with the kids, and as Vic was not going to be seeing Lily I was truly on my own now.

I still felt fine about the abortion. I almost went insane thinking about doing it beforehand, and part of me would always feel sad that my baby never was, but I knew it was for the best. I knew that if there had been any viable way for me to have that baby I would have done it, and that meant that there was nothing to feel guilty about – and I definitely acted in the best interests of the children I already have. I chose not to be swallowed up by guilt, and I would tell any woman in my situation to do that if she could. All I wanted was to make sure that I made something of my life, that I did positive things to move forward – starting with finding a home and making it lovely for me and my girls, and if I achieved that, then I could feel that my lost baby's life wasn't taken in vain.

I went for post-abortion counselling and the woman I spoke to – Tia – was great.

'Abortion is never an isolated incident,' she told me, quietly. 'There is all of your life to consider.'

I ended up telling her so much. When I tried to follow the thread of how I had got there, my memories went right back to childhood. I had been running for so long without a chance to process what had happened to me. I felt completely done in, emotionally. I kept thinking, hang on, I'm a good person – so why do bad things keep occurring?

There was no reason really, everything was so muddled up. I knew that Colin was muddled up too. He had been my white knight during such a difficult time and, now that things had settled down in terms of us splitting up, he admitted that he hated that he hadn't been able to fix everything for me.

I was still so vulnerable and I let him back in. It was only seven months since Vic had left, and I still feared he would be back. I was at a really low point.

'You're the best thing that ever happened to me,' he kept saying. 'I can't believe I've lost you. Please give me another chance.'

Basically, he wore me down.

Men like him are good at that.

Finally, I relented.

'Let's see how it goes,' I told him, cautiously. He did all the leg work. He came to see me every weekend, which was one of the ground rules, and eventually he moved beside me. The maternity leave he was covering had finished, and the only job available (he claimed) was just a few miles from where we were now living. Our relationship was going quite well by that point, but I wasn't ready to take it to the next stage, so I told him he needed to find a flat by himself, while we would stay put.

Colin wasn't too keen on us not being together, so when I found out that I was pregnant again (almost a year after the last time) he was delighted. He really regretted that he hadn't encouraged me to keep the last baby – but I wasn't so sure. By this time I'd had counselling, done an access course at college so that I could go to university and do a part-time degree – and I was working. I knew that I wanted to stick with education and this threw everything up in the air.

'This is just what we need,' Colin said. 'It's perfect – we'll be the perfect family.'

I spoke to college about it and they were supportive, but something was niggling me. Colin was so thrilled; he would be able to get time off as his job was permanent, we had more money and security than the year before, but ... I'd come to the conclusion that our relationship wasn't right. I hadn't asked him to move to where I lived – that had all come from him – and I didn't feel any excitement being with him. I really regretted that I hadn't stayed strong; I wished I'd kept him out of my life.

'We'll get a house – a four-bedroomed one,' he told me, excitedly. 'A nursery for the baby, good schools for Ruby and Lily. You can do a degree, that's fine, you can do whatever you want to do – just promise me this will work out, Megan.'

I couldn't promise him any such thing as I didn't really believe it. One day, when I was six weeks pregnant, I was weeding the garden and had this sudden, overwhelming feeling of devastation that I was pregnant. I knew without doubt that I didn't want to be tied to Colin for ever and that's what a baby would do. There would be a huge impact on me; I'd never do a degree. It washed over me and I was cold with fear.

I don't know what that all meant, the strength of that feeling, but, by teatime, when I started bleeding, I knew it was for the best. I suffered for it. I know that miscarriages are never easy, but this went on for a month. I didn't know I could bleed so much, I didn't know there could be so much pain. The bleeding would stop and start, so I kept having to go to hospital for scans to check that I really was miscarrying. Colin held on to hope, but it was obvious there was none.

I felt a sense of relief that I hadn't been in the position where I'd had to make a choice over what to do, but I wouldn't wish that sort of miscarriage on my worst enemy.

When the bleeding finally did stop and the pain faded, I became really ill. The doctors said it had gone on for far too long, and I had six months of horror. I was constantly fluey, always stricken down with viruses. It went on and on and on all winter until spring. Colin was devastated about the miscarriage but he lost patience when I was ill for so long.

We split up for good in April. He always expected the moon on a stick for birthdays and Christmas. He knew that I was unwell and had very little money, but I was aware that he wanted a good time for his fiftieth celebrations, which were coming up later that year. I was still paying for his new iPad from Christmas when he made it clear that he wanted to go away for a month to Thailand. I was so skint; I'd had no money coming in while I was a student and I needed to raise £3,000 for the trip he had set his heart on.

'I'm just not going to be able to find this money, Colin,' I admitted, on more than one occasion.

'Maybe you need to sort your priorities out then,' he'd reply.

It became ridiculous. I remember once buying Lily a Kinder egg and he went ballistic, telling me he'd never get to Thailand if I kept wasting my money! Eventually, I scraped enough money together to rent a house in the Highlands for a few days. I'd tried to come up with lots of suggestions and promised that we could do Thailand when my student loan came through the following year, but it was never enough. Even the trip to Scotland seemed to make him think I had come up with a terrible insult. Behind my back, he made plans to go away with one of his friends without me, which was the final straw. I called it off – for good this time.

He pestered me for a bit, but I didn't buckle. He finally moved away and I felt I could get on with my life.

CHAPTER 15

ONCE UPON A TIME

February 2012 – present day

My court case was disjointed because I had moved, and was still moving, around – I had three different solicitors. The court process always follows the resident parent so it went with me, and to various courts. There was no continuity of legal representation for me and I always felt like I was starting from scratch with each one, having to prove that I wasn't making this up. As it was such an extreme case, I needed a barrister as well as a solicitor, but the barrister kept changing. At the second hearing, I remember the new one reading the documents in front of me. She was silent for a while, then she closed the folder, looked at me and said, 'Well, one of you is mad – I just don't know which one yet.' She was horrible, but she was just saying what so many people thought. I was the one coming out with all this stuff; Vic was claiming it was all a figment of my imagination. It was only once I managed to regain access to my old Facebook account, about a year into the court process – and all of the messages between me and all the characters that Vic had created backed up exactly what I had been claiming – that I began to be taken seriously. Vic still denied that any of it was true, claiming that I had written all of the messages myself. Luckily, the third solicitor I had, who worked on my case for nearly two years in the end, was brilliant. She worked tirelessly. It was such a complicated and unusual case to unravel, and it was thanks to her that things finally got moving in the right direction. She found me an amazing barrister, who was sensitive, kind and fantastic at her job, and who also stayed on my case almost until the end. Because of the seriousness of what Vic had done, it was decided by the court that the social worker would become Lily's guardian within the court process, which meant that Lily had her own solicitor too. Both the social worker and Lily's solicitor were lovely, and, like me, had Lily's best interests at heart. I felt very fortunate to have such great professionals on our side.

In June 2013 Vic tried to withdraw from the court process. He had been backed into a corner, being asked to provide details that were impossible for him to give, such as the full names and addresses of all of the characters he had created. He realised his game was over, but rather than tell the truth he chose to give up any chance of seeing his daughter. However, the judge refused his application to withdraw, stating that because of the seriousness of what had happened the case needed to be concluded. Vic didn't come to court again after that, but technically he was still part of the proceedings, and was sent any documents that were raised.

One thing that was interesting in court was when the judge ordered the court papers from Zack's case to be disclosed. There was some truth in that story. After Vic physically attacked her, Zack's mum fought tooth and nail to keep him away from her son. There were some striking similarities between things he did to me and things he did to her, but despite being a very intelligent woman she didn't have the amount of evidence that I did to be able to protect her son. At that time the internet was still fairly primitive, so Vic's ways of tormenting her were done in 'real life' rather than cyberspace, and unfortunately that didn't leave a trail. With Vic being the accomplished liar that he was, he managed to get his own way in court and have access to Zack. It turns out that Zack died not because she was negligent, as Vic made out; it was just a tragic accident. My heart goes out to her to this day.

In July 2013, with Vic and me giving completely different accounts of what had happened, there was a 'fact-finding' investigation by the authorities to determine what the reality of the situation was. I wished them well with it – at times, I was still unsure myself about what was real and what was a figment of Vic's imagination. I was terrified about what the outcome would be; not because I had ever lied or embellished matters, but because there were now other people involved in deciding what kind of future would be there for me and the girls. When it was published, I felt nothing but relief. They stated:

'It would be easy to underestimate the risk Mr Morana poses as he hasn't physically assaulted Ms Henley or Lily, but he has the capacity to do so as evidenced in the police papers. Mr Morana physically assaulted his previous partner and the photographic evidence certainly highlights it was not a "slap" as he claims.

'Mr Morana did not return Lily as agreed after a direct contact and I am in no doubt from reading the police papers and texts to Ms Henley that this was another incident of Mr Morana trying to control and terrify Ms Henley with no consideration as to the impact on his daughter. I am therefore of the opinion that Mr Morana poses a risk of abducting Lily in the future.

'Mr Morana has made Ms Henley live, for a number of years, in fear of her life and Lily's. He hassled her to believe that there was a murder in her yard, that people were out to murder her and Lily, that he was a contract killer, and he stalked her through the internet. These are only the bare minimum of the behaviours demonstrated by Mr Morana that will have been hugely psychologically damaging to Ms Henley.

'The Fact Finding judgement is clear that Mr Morana appears to be a pathological liar who suffers from a dissocial personality disorder.

'My concern would be Mr Morana's capacity to show empathy for his daughter or understand how psychologically damaging his behaviour is to her. Lily has already suffered significant harm emotionally as I'm in no doubt Mr Morana's behaviour impacted hugely on Ms Henley's emotional well-being; which would have had a detrimental impact on her capacity to parent Lily.

'The risks are also highlighted by the fact that Mr Morana does not accept the harm he has caused and shows no insight into the impact of his behaviour. In fact, I am of the view his priority has been to control and manipulate Ms Henley and make a fantasy world of violence rather than having any concern for Lily's well-being …

'I am of the view that Mr Morana's wish to have contact with Lily has been driven by his motivation to continue to control Ms Henley and abuse her emotionally.

'I personally have never worked another case where the amount of psychological abuse was to this extent. Mr Morana has used the fear of murder of his then partner and daughter to control Ms Henley. In my opinion his actions, manipulation and web of extreme deceit make Mr Morana a very dangerous man to any partner or child as he has no consideration or compassion for the trauma his actions cause.'

The judge, calling it 'a most complicated and difficult case ... the most bizarre case I have come across', also accepted my version of events:

'I formed the view that she is an entirely honest witness who has been, to use a colloquialism, suckered into this situation. She used the word "played". This is what I think happened. She used the word "conditioned". That is what I think happened. She was groomed by this man: I have no doubt about that at all on any standard of proof ... He concocted this identity, he concocted identities for others. She said, "It was safer for me to believe him rather than not," and she was in fear, put in fear by him, at risk of being killed and Lily being killed by his gypsy relatives.'

The judge concluded that I was telling the truth 100 per cent. I had taken the stand for two full hours earlier that day to give evidence, and had an awful migraine from the stress, but I could have screamed for joy after he made that comment. The barrister came over, hugged me, and apologised for ever doubting what I'd said.

'To be honest,' I told her, 'any sane person would!'

'Never feel stupid for being taken in by him,' she said. 'It could have happened to anyone. He's *that* good.'

I'd always felt that. I'd never felt like a mug, because it was a full-time job for him, and he was very, very clever.

That was not the end of the legal process, however. There were further hearings, and by the summer of 2014 the court case had been dragging on for two and a half years, over eighteen different hearings. It was like a millstone around my neck. The work I had to do for it took up most of my time, and I hated living with the uncertainty of not knowing whether I would ever truly be free of Vic. He'd not been allowed to see Lily since kidnapping her in 2012, but occasionally sent presents and cards through my solicitor.

The final hearing was scheduled for July 2014. Vic had decided that he would like to attend, to everyone's surprise, although he would have no legal representation due to no longer being entitled to Legal Aid. It was agreed because of the distance he would have to travel, and because he claimed his autism (that he most likely doesn't actually have) would make it hard for him to be in that environment, that he would be able to appear by video link. I was relieved that I wouldn't have to be in the same room as him. Disaster struck a few days before when my barrister gave my solicitor the news that she would be unable to make the case because she was stuck in the High Court on another case which had overrun. My solicitor stepped up yet again, and at the eleventh hour found a perfect last-minute replacement. Felicity was incredibly glamorous, a beautiful woman who had just the experience I needed to win people over.

I was stunned in court when Felicity managed to pull out the salient details from two and a half years of court papers over one weekend. Her style in court was a lot more aggressive than my other barrister, which I think was exactly what was needed.

No one really expected Vic to actually turn up to the court hearing. I was sitting in a side room with my solicitor and barrister, when a court usher came in to tell us Vic was at court in Cardiff, ready to appear by video link. I crumbled. I starting shaking and crying. By now it had been over eighteen months since I'd seen him, and I'd come so far emotionally in that time.

'You don't have to go into the courtroom if you don't want to,' my barrister said, but I didn't know which would be worse – seeing him, or waiting outside not knowing what was happening. Eventually the social worker talked me into going in, but screens were put up so I wouldn't have to look at the screen he would appear on.

Over the next two days in court Vic was pretty much ripped apart by my barrister and Lily's solicitor. He was still unable to accept that he had lied about anything, or that he had caused me or my children any harm. The judge finally gave his verdict, and granted the orders that prevented Vic from having any contact whatsoever with Lily for her entire childhood, and also an order preventing him from making any further application to the court, without seeking prior approval from the court to do so. His parental responsibility was also discharged. For a few moments I felt elated that, after such a long slog, I had got the result that I wanted and that Lily needed to keep her safe. I felt like I was floating. The judge then asked Vic if he had anything to say.

Naturally, he did.

I couldn't resist peering round the edge of the screen to see how he was reacting to all of this.

'I don't care what you say. You can't stop me from seeing my daughter. I'll see her; don't you worry about that,' he threatened, then angrily pushed his chair back and disappeared off the screen.

I was straight back to feeling dark and hopeless. My guts were churning with fear – the way I'd felt during my time with him came rushing back again and I hated it. I would never be free of him. I felt sure that he would find some way to get at me, to get at Lily. I knew by now that he wasn't a gypsy with connections, but I also knew that he was both very clever and extremely unhinged. During the court process, independent psychiatric assessments were done, and they concluded that he most likely had an antisocial personality disorder, which I'm told is the new, politically correct way of saying 'psychopath'.

My legal team (and Lily's), who knew me so well by this point, understood how I would be feeling after Vic's parting shot. As we left the courtroom, they tried to reassure me that I would be OK, that we were as protected as we could possibly be. I wanted to scream – *I don't care! As long as he is out there, I'll never really feel safe.*

My only solace was that he would go straight to prison for breaching any of the court orders if he did come close. The police put extra security on my house, but I still felt that he was capable of anything, and I knew he would hate the fact that I had won.

I didn't actually feel that it was a case of winning, though. I did what I had to do to protect my cubs, but there was no sense of personal satisfaction about it. In a way, as much as I hated him for what he put us through, I still felt sorry for him. Without disclosing confidential details from court, I did find out from his medical records that Vic's childhood was certainly not a happy one. Some pretty bad stuff must have happened to make him into the person he is today, capable of so much evil. But at the same time I realised that his personality disorder is one that is near impossible to cure, especially when he is not even close to accepting that he has done anything wrong. I think back to things that he did, like the advert with my full name and address on an adult website, inviting anyone to come and have sex with me. He did that knowing that his own baby daughter was in the house, and that by doing so he could be putting her at any kind of risk. Those are not the actions of a father who cares about his child. It's also pretty sad that he felt like he had to pretend to be a superstar DJ, to be able to get people to like him and respect him.

Most of all I feel sad for Lily. She is five now and doesn't understand why she doesn't have a dad. She sees Ruby going to stay with Lucas, and wonders why she doesn't do the same. Upon the advice of the social worker I sometimes show her pictures of him, and talk about her 'tummy daddy'. I tell her he is not well and that's why he can't see her. As she gets older and more curious, I will tell her more of the story in an age-appropriate way. I worry about the effect on her, though, when she realises what he did to us. She is such a gorgeous little girl, still a handful, but so clever and funny. My family all love her, she is such a character. She does look a lot like her dad, especially her eyes, which is sometimes hard, but she is mine and I wouldn't change her for the world. I am both parents to her, and I will never let her down.

I never saw the whole picture until it was too late. It had been such a gradual, slow thing over such a long period of time. Vic had put so much effort into making it all believable, to build on real-life events, and he was so clever that I don't really feel stupid for falling for it – it could happen to anyone. To have kept all those lies going for so long – and to simultaneously 'be' all the different characters he created … well, that takes some doing. He never messed up, not once. People have often said that he is a genius, and I agree; I only wish that he put his abilities into something constructive, not destructive. If someone put that much effort, that much time, into creating another world, creating multiple people, creating another entire story … can you honestly say you would have noticed immediately? If so, I'd love to know what I did wrong, why he thought I deserved to have my life turned upside down. He fooled so many people – psychiatrists, police, everyone. He was in it for the long game. He was torturing me for such a while, I went through years of this, years of unnecessary stress while I was pregnant with Lily, while I was having no sleep with the baby; I was still the mother of his child, no matter what else had been going on, but he was perfectly willing to keep playing me all that time. What I can't really forgive is that I was frightened to bond with my own little girl. I would hold her close to me and worry that it might be the last time. I thought about running away, but where would I go? I didn't really have the money to go to somewhere like Australia, but I was also led to believe that there was no hiding place. There was a worldwide network of murdering gypsies out there, and they would track me and my girls down no matter where we were. Nowhere was safe, there was nowhere to run to.

My story is a warning, a story for our times. It's a cautionary tale, a reminder that not everyone is who they claim to be, not everything is what it seems.

I know that people will judge me. Hopefully, they'll understand by the time they read it all, but I'm sure there will times when they will shake their heads, perhaps even shout as the story unfolds, and think I was stupid or naïve or gullible.

And I can guarantee they will be thinking that they'd never fall for it.

Guess what?

I'd have thought that too – before it happened to me.

I was smart, I was sorted. I was streetwise, positive, happy-go-lucky. I'd had a lot of crap to deal with but I was striving to make my life better and I always had time for anyone down on their luck. I'd had some difficult times, but haven't we all? I was educated, self-sufficient, a nice middle-class young woman from a good family. It didn't matter. I fell for it, and my life will never be the same again.

I never really lost my fighting spirit, and that kept me going. When I met Colin I was dejected and I did think I needed to just accept how things were, but I pulled myself out of it. There did come that point where I thought, 'Sod you, Vic; I'm not going to live my life like this any more, because it's no life.' I did think I would rather take the consequences because I was sick of being controlled.

This was domestic abuse in a really extreme, psychological form. There is no such thing as a stereotypical victim. People have this idea of the 'sort' of woman who might be a prime candidate, but that's nonsense. At the time, I couldn't explain to people what was going on; now that it's over, a few of my close friends know what happened, but the bulk of people have no idea. Where would I begin?

I'm still at university and working hard to make a better future for me and my girls. It's not easy studying with two kids to look after, but I've finished my first year with good grades. I'm also still running my business, which is going well. I certainly don't have time to get bored! I got rehoused because of the danger we were in from Vic and we've had to rebuild our lives, and get to know people in a new area. It's taken a while but I finally feel like we are settled, and have made some good friends, particularly one of my neighbours who I spend many a night with, drinking wine and putting the world to rights. I still struggle with depression; I have good days and bad days. When everything's OK

I'm fine, but if problems start cropping up in life I don't cope as well as I used to; it's like all my coping reserves were depleted by Vic. But I feel like I'm moving forward, and, as more time passes, the whole thing with Vic seems more and more surreal and like a bad dream. If it wasn't for my little reminder in the form of Lily I would wonder if it ever actually happened.

I don't have a man in my life and I'm happy that way. I enjoy the calm of being single, to be honest. I have more than enough to fill my time, with the girls, university and work, so I don't have a chance to feel lonely. I don't have trust issues, weirdly enough, because I realise that Vic really was one of a kind, there's not too many like him floating around. I like just being a little family of three, me and the girls. The three of us recently spent a month travelling in Thailand, which was amazing. We stayed in some beautiful places, met some great people, saw pink dolphins, went scuba diving and rode elephants. I wanted to give the girls some happy memories that they'd keep for ever. Maxie's still here too; he's getting quite old now, but he is great for a cuddle and the only man I need! That's my life – and I'm happy with it.

I won't lie – this has all been so very hard. People often say that they can't believe I'm such a positive person, that I smile so much, when they know what's happened to me. But I have always believed that you can only control your reactions to things, not what other people do to you. If I stopped smiling, if I stopped laughing, Vic would have won. I'll never let that happen.

There are some things you can predict in life. You might not know when they'll happen but they're guaranteed. You'll lose people you love. You'll meet others that steal your heart. You'll be unbearably sad and immeasurably happy. I've had all of that. But how in the world could I have imagined what Vic would bring into my world?

I've learned some harsh lessons, in a very unusual way, but I'm a stronger person for it. I know that I won't let this stop me trusting people – of course I'm sometimes wary, but I believe that most people are good, and that I'm a decent human being too; it just so happened that my world collided with a man who decided to do all he could to wreck it. If I allowed him that power, if I allowed him that sort of control, what type of message would I be sending to my girls? That you don't have a say over how your life will be? That someone can come along and determine what the rest of your limited time on this planet will be like?

No.

I won't be a victim.

They'll have the life I always wanted for them. It will be full of laughter and love, we'll dance and we'll sing, we'll trust people and we'll be happy. He is the father of one of my darling daughters, and that is a gift he can never take back. I wouldn't be without her for the world – so, with that alone, Vic Morana has actually given me a wonderful thing.

I think back to the early days when he was so nice to me, when the way he called me 'Miss Henley' warmed my heart and made me think I'd found someone I could spend my life with. I need to hold on to any good moments there were, because the other moments, the dark ones of thinking I was going to die, that my children would be killed, that my life was one of violence and danger, are something I never want to think of again. None of us knows what's coming, so why dwell on the bad stuff?

Writing this book has been so cathartic – and now, now that I've told the world, it's time to move on from it as much as I can. There will be more court cases, of that I'm sure – Vic won't let this lie. There will be harder questions as Lily gets older. There will be nights when I hear a noise as I fall asleep, or think a door has just banged, and my imagination will run away with me.

I'm strong and I'm happy. I have my girls, and I have a life full of incredible things.

Miss Henley has a bright, beautiful future ahead of her – and the world is a wonderful place.

But … just one thing … I would love it if everyone who has read my story would be very, very careful of butterflies flapping their wings online – because, after all, you never know who's really out there ☺

ACKNOWLEDGEMENTS

There are so many people to thank!

When the rug has been well and truly pulled out from under your feet and your life is turned completely upside down, you find out who is really there for you. The first person I have to thank is J, the best friend anyone could ever ask for. She's been there for me through thick and thin over the last twenty-four years, from being pony-mad ten-year-olds to now sensible(ish) mums in our mid-thirties, and everything in between. J, you really have kept me sane throughout all this. I don't know what I'd have done without our daily phone calls and your calm voice of reason. Thank you for never judging me and always being there.

I need to thank my family too, particularly Mum, for helping me to pick up the pieces of my life and rebuild myself, emotionally, physically and financially. A lot of people don't have that support and I'm truly grateful, and sorry for everything I've put you through over the years!

I was incredibly lucky to have the legal team that I had. My solicitor worked tirelessly on my case, often during evenings and weekends to get things done. I think she almost became as invested in the case as I was, and she says it's definitely one she will remember until the day she dies. Thank you so much for taking charge of the situation and navigating my case in the right direction; I appreciate that was not an easy task given the circumstances. Our last phone call felt like the end of an era. Another thing to thank my solicitor for is bringing my barristers to the case. They were exactly the right people for the job; excellent at what they do and their warmth and empathy got me through the more difficult court appearances. Also many thanks to the solicitor who represented my daughter – you are lovely and I could not have asked for anyone better for her. Thank you all so much for believing me and supporting me through some incredibly stressful times.

A huge thanks to Lily's guardian from CAFCASS, who was the first person who gave me any hope that I would be able to keep my daughter safe. Together with the student on placement with her, she soon found who was the credible one in the situation, and her evidence in court was what convinced the judge to hand out very rarely given court orders to keep Lily safe. Social workers get so much flak, but these two people were both amazing. Like me they had Lily's welfare and best interests at heart, and it was their intervention which inspired me to go back into education myself.

Thanks also to Colin: although things didn't work out between us long term, you without a doubt lifted me out of a horrendous situation, when most people would have walked on by. You were my knight in shining armour and I wish you all the best.

This whole experience has definitely changed me and I'm a bit of a hermit these days, but I am lucky to have friends aside from J who are always there for me and regularly check in to see how I'm doing. Dear friends – thanks for getting me through some dark times and still being there on the other side.

And of course I have to thank my two wonderful daughters, who always give me a reason to smile and carry on. I'm a lucky Mumma. One day you will be old enough to read this and hopefully you will understand why sometimes things haven't been perfect. I love you both so much and I will always do my best for you.

Thanks to David Riding at MBA Literary Agency. Also to Kate Latham and the team at HarperCollins – I don't even know who some of you are, but thank you so much for all of your help and expertise.

I can hardly believe that I am looking at all of this written down. There have been some dark days, far too many of them, and I don't really know what lies ahead, but it has been so cathartic to tell my story, to see it all in black and white and think, 'That really happened – and I survived it.'